bills open kitchen

For Natalie, Edie and Inès

Thank you to Kay for her vision and guidance, patience and even temperament; Petrina and Marcus for their dedication, concentration and for creating inspired beauty with our extraordinary images; Briget for her stress-free cooking, sense of humour and onion and feta tart; Marylouise for pulling together all the facets into a beautiful book; Victoria Carey for her hard work despite the tight deadlines; Jane for her rigorous food editing and testing and flexibility with the restraints of my availability; Wendy Quisumbing and Rebecca Truda for supporting Jane in testing; Diana Thompson for her final once over; Linda Dayan for letting us have run of her cottage; Trent Nathan for allowing us to capture the magic of the Pittwater; a special big thank you to my hard-working and committed team back at the restaurants on whom my family and I rely so heavily—Kath, Andy, Sophie and Nicole and everyone else; Juliet for her strength and accessibility; Amanda who takes my books into the world with incredible energy and enthusiasm, and finally Natalie, the other half of the "Bill" everyone knows, who makes me write recipes when I'd much rather be cooking and playing with the girls.

Photographer: Petrina Tinslay
Art director and designer: Marylouise Brammer
Creative Consultant and Stylist: Marcus Hay
Food Stylist: Bill Granger
Home Economist and Food Stylist: Briget Palmer
Editorial Project Manager: Victoria Carey
Food Editor: Jane Lawson

Originally published in Australia in 2003 by Murdoch Books Pty Limited

FIRST U.S. EDITION PUBLISHED 2004

Library of Congress Cataloging-in-Publication Data is available.

ISBN 0-06-074048-5

05 06 07 08 09   10 9 8 7 6 5 4 3 2 1

Printed in China by 1010 Printing Limited.

bills open kitchen

by bill granger

photography by petrina tinslay

WILLIAM MORROW

An Imprint of HarperCollins*Publishers*

contents

'On a recent holiday in Paris, I had the luxury of shopping daily at local markets, buying some of the most beautiful produce I've ever seen—blueberries with flavour, pink and white radishes the size of my little finger, just-picked herbs and salad greens, amazing cheeses that just oozed—really extraordinary. We spent time planning and cooking meals, day after day.

'While I'd love to be able to shop and cook like this every day, it's not realistic given my increasingly busy life. Sometimes there's barely enough time for a quick trip to the supermarket, but I never let this become a barrier to cooking, or let the job of preparing dinner every day become tedious.

'When cooking is beginning to feel like a chore, I try to make it as pleasurable as possible by trying new and interesting things. It's the way I maintain my passion. My daughter Edie's first word was yum, a reminder to me that food should be more than just fuel. It must be absolutely delicious!

'I adore pleasing people and food is a sure-fire way to anyone's heart. Preparing a meal for family and friends is a way I share my love and gives me time to reflect, concentrate and create—while getting lots of compliments. But the demands of modern life and cooking with hungry children hovering often prevents me from spending as much time cooking as I would like. So I've developed a way of cooking that fits in with the shape of my life now. It's fast, fresh and flavoursome, and much simpler. I'm always thinking about what things I can leave out without sacrificing flavour. It's all about making things as easy as possible in the kitchen. "Less is more" sums it up.

'This book was written in a mad household with a two-year-old, a two-month-old and two sleep-deprived parents.

'I hope you enjoy my new recipes.'

Bill

breakfast

breakfast

'I'm annoyingly chirpy in the morning. I'm naturally a morning person and usually find that what I don't get done by lunchtime, doesn't get done at all. Many people sacrifice breakfast in the struggle to keep up with the fast pace of life. But I always make an effort to have breakfast with my family. We usually all decide on our breakfast, whether it be buckwheat pancakes or soft-boiled eggs or whatever, and we all share in its preparation while getting ready for the day. When we're rushed, which seems to be quite often in our crazy household, our standby breakfast is the homemade muesli I keep in the pantry for just such occasions, served with fresh fruit and yoghurt. One of my life's greatest luxuries is to be able to sit quietly reading the newspaper over a cup of coffee, which doesn't happen nearly enough! Breakfast is my favourite meal of the day, partly because it's the only meal you can justify eating in bed.'

bills eggs

fried

2 teaspoons olive oil
2 eggs, at room temperature
sea salt
freshly ground black pepper

Place a large non-stick frying pan over a medium to high heat for 1 minute. Add the olive oil and swirl until the base of the pan is evenly coated. Carefully crack two eggs into the pan and sprinkle with salt and pepper. Cook for a minute. If you like the yolks of your eggs harder, cover the pan with a lid and cook for another minute. Serve with sourdough or wholemeal toast and simple spiced tomato relish (page 151).

scrambled

2 eggs, at room temperature
80 ml (1/3 cup) cream
a pinch of salt
10 g (1/4 oz) butter

Place the eggs, cream and salt in a bowl and whisk together. Put the butter in a non-stick frying pan over a high heat. Once the butter is melted, pour in the egg mixture and cook for 20 seconds, or until it begins to set around the edge. Using a wooden spoon, stir and bring the egg mixture on the edge of the pan into the centre. It is important to fold the eggs, not scramble them. Leave for 20 seconds, then repeat the folding process. When the eggs are just set, turn out onto a plate and serve with sourdough or wholemeal toast.

boiled

Place a saucepan of water over a high heat and bring to the boil. Gently place your eggs, which should be at room temperature, into the water then adjust the heat until the water is simmering. For a soft-boiled egg, cook for 4 minutes, medium-boiled 5 to 6 minutes and hard-boiled 10 minutes.

poached

Fill a shallow frying pan with water until it is 5 cm (2 inches) deep and place over a high heat. Once the water boils, turn off the heat and break the eggs directly into the water. Crack the shells open at the water surface so the eggs simply slide into the water. Cover with a tight-fitting lid and leave to cook for 3 minutes, or until the egg whites are opaque. Remove from the pan with a slotted spoon and drain on a clean tea towel.

bills breakfast sides

garlic mushrooms

20 g (3/4 oz) butter
1 garlic clove, finely chopped
500 g (1 lb 2 oz) mushrooms, halved
sea salt
freshly ground black pepper

Place the butter and garlic in a saucepan over a medium to high heat. Add the mushrooms, 60 ml (1/4 cup) water and salt and pepper. Cover and cook, stirring occasionally, for about 15 minutes, or until the mushrooms are cooked and the liquid is syrupy.

roast tomatoes

8 small tomatoes (I leave the tops attached as they look better)
2 tablespoons extra virgin olive oil
sea salt
freshly ground black pepper

Preheat the oven to 200°C (400°F/Gas 6). Place the tomatoes in a small ovenproof dish. Drizzle with olive oil and add the salt and pepper. Cook for 30 minutes, then leave to cool for 10 minutes before serving.

crispy potatoes

600 g (1 lb 5 oz) potatoes, peeled and diced into 2 cm (3/4 inch) cubes
2 tablespoons olive oil
sea salt
freshly ground black pepper

Preheat the oven to 200°C (400°F/Gas 6). Place the potatoes and olive oil in a bowl and toss well until the potatoes are evenly coated. Put on a baking tray and bake for 30 minutes, or until golden and crispy. Remove from the oven, place in a serving bowl and season to taste with salt and pepper.

bacon curls

8 long thin rashers streaky bacon, rind removed

Preheat the oven to 200°C (400°F/Gas 6). Wrap each rasher of bacon around two fingers to form a curl. Put the curled rashers upright in a baking tray. Place in the oven and cook for 20 minutes, or until crispy.

All side dishes serve 4

The secret to a lovely light pancake is to fold the egg whites through the batter in two batches and remember to always use a metal spoon so as not to deflate the mixture.

buckwheat pancakes with fresh blueberries and maple syrup

165 g (1¹/4 cups) buckwheat flour
60 g (¹/2 cup) plain (all-purpose) flour
1 teaspoon baking powder
2 teaspoons caster (superfine) sugar
a pinch of salt
4 eggs, separated
500 ml (2 cups) buttermilk
butter, for greasing the pan
310 g (2 cups) blueberries

to serve
plain yoghurt
2 mangoes, cheeked and scored
maple syrup

Preheat the oven to 120°C (250°F/Gas 1). Place the buckwheat flour, plain flour, baking powder, sugar and salt in a bowl and stir to combine. Place the egg yolks and buttermilk in another bowl and stir well to combine. Add the buttermilk mixture to the flour and mix lightly until just combined. A few lumps are fine, so do not overmix. Place the egg whites in a clean, dry stainless steel bowl and whisk until stiff peaks form. Using a large metal spoon, fold the egg whites through the batter in two batches.

Heat a large non-stick frying pan over a medium heat and brush a small portion of butter over the base. For each pancake, ladle 4 tablespoons of batter into the pan and sprinkle with a heaped tablespoon of blueberries. Cook for about 2 minutes, or until bubbles appear on the surface of the pancake. Turn the pancakes over and cook for another minute. Transfer to a plate and keep warm in the oven while you make the remaining pancakes.

Serve the pancakes in stacks of three with the yoghurt, mango and a jug of maple syrup. Makes 12

fresh baked beans

2 tablespoons olive oil
2 x 400 g (14 oz) cans cannellini beans
1 garlic clove, sliced
1/2 teaspoon chilli flakes
1 small red onion, sliced into thin wedges
250 g (1 punnet) cherry tomatoes

to serve
1 teaspoon olive oil
8 slices prosciutto
1 tablespoon fresh oregano leaves

Preheat the oven to 200°C (400°F/Gas 6). Place the olive oil, beans, garlic, chilli flakes, onion and tomatoes in a small baking dish and stir to combine. Loosely cover with foil and bake for 25 to 30 minutes, or until the onion is tender and the tomatoes slightly shrivelled. Meanwhile, heat 1 teaspoon of olive oil in a large frying pan over a medium to high heat and cook the prosciutto until lightly crisp. Remove and place on paper towels. Serve the baked beans sprinkled with fresh oregano leaves and the crisp prosciutto. Serves 4

To make raspberry swirl yoghurt, just mash 1/2 cup of raspberries with a fork and lightly ripple through a cup of plain yoghurt.

blueberry and almond toasted muesli

300 g (3 cups) rolled oats
125 ml (1/2 cup) apple juice
2 tablespoons vegetable oil
80 g (1/2 cup) raw almonds
125 g (1 cup) sunflower seeds
40 g (1/4 cup) pumpkin seeds (pepitas)
40 g (1/4 cup) sesame seeds
30 g (1/2 cup) flaked coconut
125 g (1 cup) dried blueberries (if you can't get these, use currants or sultanas or
  a mixture of both)

to serve
raspberry swirl yoghurt (above)
nectarines, sliced
milk

Preheat the oven to 160°C (315°F/Gas 2–3). Place all the ingredients, except for the dried blueberries, in a large bowl and stir well to combine. Spread the mixture evenly over a large baking tray and place in the oven for 30 minutes, stirring occasionally until lightly browned. Remove from the oven, allow to cool then add the blueberries. This muesli can be stored in an airtight container for up to a month. Serve with the raspberry swirl yoghurt, nectarines and milk. Serves 4

coconut pancakes with banana and passionfruit syrup

215 g (1³/4 cups) plain (all-purpose) flour
1 teaspoon baking powder
1 tablespoon caster (superfine) sugar
65 g (³/4 cup) desiccated coconut
a pinch of salt
4 eggs, separated
250 ml (1 cup) milk

250 ml (1 cup) coconut milk
50 g (1³/4 oz) unsalted butter, melted
butter, for greasing the pan

to serve
6 bananas, sliced in half lengthways
passionfruit syrup (below)

Preheat the oven to 120°C (250°F/Gas 1). Place the flour, baking powder, sugar, desiccated coconut and salt in a bowl and stir to combine. Place the egg yolks, milk and coconut milk into another bowl and whisk to combine. Add the milk mixture and butter to the dry ingredients and mix lightly with a metal spoon until just combined.

Place the egg whites in a clean, dry stainless steel bowl and whisk until stiff peaks form. Using a large metal spoon, fold the egg whites through the batter in two batches.

Heat a large non-stick frying pan over a medium heat and brush a small portion of butter over the base. For each pancake, drop 3 tablespoons of batter into the pan. Avoid overcrowding the pan with pancakes. Cook for 2 minutes on one side, turn and cook for another minute. Transfer to a plate and keep warm in the oven while you make the remaining pancakes.

Serve the pancakes in stacks of three with the banana and passionfruit syrup. Makes 18

passionfruit syrup

115 g (¹/2 cup) caster (superfine) sugar
60 g (¹/4 cup) passionfruit pulp

Combine the sugar, passionfruit pulp and 125 ml (¹/2 cup) water in a small saucepan over a medium heat and bring to the boil, skimming any scum from the surface. Reduce the heat to low and simmer for 10 minutes. Remove from the heat and set aside to cool.

turkish eggs

250 g (1 cup) plain yoghurt
1 garlic clove, crushed, optional
a pinch of sea salt
freshly ground black pepper
4 eggs
1 tablespoon extra virgin olive oil
1 teaspoon paprika
50 g (1 handful) baby English spinach leaves

Preheat the oven to 180°C (350°F/Gas 4). Place the yoghurt and garlic in a small bowl and stir to combine. Season with salt and pepper. Divide between four small ovenproof dishes and place in the oven for 10 minutes.

While the yoghurt is warming, place 5 cm (2 inches) of water in a deep frying pan and bring to the boil. Turn off the heat and immediately break the eggs into the pan. To stop the egg whites spreading too much, break the eggs directly into the water, carefully opening the shells at the water surface so that the eggs slide into the water. Cover the pan with a tight-fitting lid. Leave to cook undisturbed in the water for about 3 minutes. The eggs are cooked when the whites are opaque. Remove from the pan with a slotted spoon and drain on a clean tea towel.

Mix the olive oil and paprika together in a small bowl. Season with salt and pepper. Remove the yoghurt from the oven and top with the spinach leaves and poached egg. Drizzle over the olive oil mixture and serve at once. Serves 4

When fresh peaches are out of season you can use
dried peaches or other dried fruit by soaking them
in boiling water for 5 minutes.

five-grain porridge with brown sugar peaches

250 g (2¹/2 cups) of mixed grains such as rolled oats, rolled rice, rolled barley,
   triticale or kibbled rye
600 ml (2¹/2 cups) boiling water
600 ml (2¹/2 cups) milk
3 peaches, quartered
80 g (¹/3 cup) brown sugar

to serve
brown sugar, extra
warmed milk

Preheat the oven to 200°C (400°F/Gas 6). Place the grains and boiling water in a saucepan
and stir to combine. Leave for 10 minutes. Add the milk and stir again. Place over a medium
heat and slowly bring to the boil. Reduce the heat and simmer for 10 minutes, stirring often.

Meanwhile, place the peaches on a baking tray and sprinkle with the brown sugar. Bake in
the oven for about 15 minutes, or until the fruit has softened and slightly caramelized.

Spoon the porridge into serving bowls and top with the peaches. Serve with brown sugar
and a jug of warmed milk. Serves 4

Some health food shops sell a five-grain mix which I think is ideal for this porridge.
Triticale is an interesting grain which is a cross between rye and wheat and gives a
delicious nutty flavour. Make up more than you need of the grain mix and store in an
airtight container for up to 2 months.

ham and gruyère french toast

4 eggs
185 ml (3/4 cup) milk
sea salt
freshly ground black pepper
4 slices white bread, 3 cm (11/4 inch) thick
2 teaspoons Dijon mustard
4 slices leg ham, trimmed to fit bread
4 slices Gruyère cheese, trimmed to fit bread
1 tablespoon olive oil

Preheat the oven to 180°C (350°F/Gas 4). Place the eggs, milk, salt and pepper into a large bowl. Whisk to combine. Season with salt and pepper.

With a sharp, thin-bladed knife, carefully slit open one side of each slice of bread to form a pocket, leaving 1 cm (1/2 inch) around the edges. Spread the mustard on one side of the pocket and place a slice of ham and cheese inside. Put the pockets into a shallow dish. Pour over the egg mixture and leave for 5 minutes, turning once.

Heat a non-stick frying pan over a medium to high heat, add half of the olive oil and swirl to coat the base of the pan. Add two bread pockets, cook on one side for about 2 minutes until golden brown, turn and cook for another minute. Remove from the pan and place on a baking tray. Repeat with the remaining oil and bread pockets. Place the baking tray in the oven and cook for 10 minutes, or until cooked in the centre. Serves 4

simple sweetcorn cakes with avocado salsa

525 g (2²/₃ cups) fresh corn kernels, cut
   from 3 large corn cobs
1 small red onion, chopped
2 eggs
15 g (¹/₂ cup) chopped coriander (cilantro)
   leaves
125 g (1 cup) plain (all-purpose) flour
1 teaspoon baking powder

sea salt
freshly ground black pepper
vegetable oil, for frying

to serve
avocado salsa (below)

Preheat the oven to 120°C (250°F/Gas 1). Place 2 cups of the corn kernels and the onion, eggs, coriander, flour, baking powder, salt and pepper in a food processor and process until combined. Place in a large bowl, add the remaining corn and stir to combine.

Heat 1 tablespoon of the vegetable oil in a non-stick frying pan over a medium to high heat. When the oil is hot, drop 2 heaped tablespoons of mixture per sweetcorn cake into the pan and cook in batches of three for 1 minute each side. Drain on paper towels and keep warm in the oven while you are making the rest of the cakes. Serve with the avocado salsa. Makes 12

avocado salsa

2 ripe avocados, stones removed and diced
15 g (¹/₂ cup) coriander (cilantro) leaves
2 tablespoons lime or lemon juice
2 tablespoons finely chopped spring onions
   (scallions)

dash Tabasco sauce, optional
sea salt
freshly ground black pepper

Place all the ingredients in a bowl and stir very gently to combine.

All these spreads are delicious served with fresh
brioche or crusty bread and will keep up to a week
if stored in an airtight container and refrigerated.

chocolate spread

200 g (7 oz) dark chocolate
125 ml (1/2 cup) cream
30 g (1/4 cup) ground hazelnuts

Place the chocolate and cream in a heatproof bowl over a saucepan of simmering water,
making sure the bowl does not touch the water. Stir until the chocolate has just melted,
then remove from the heat and stir through the ground hazelnuts. Leave to cool until
smooth enough to spread.

ricotta spread

125 g (1/2 cup) ricotta
125 g (1/2 cup) creamy yoghurt
1 tablespoon caster (superfine) sugar
1 vanilla bean (I also use 1 teaspoon of natural vanilla extract instead)

Place the ricotta, yoghurt and sugar in a bowl. Scrape the seeds from the vanilla bean into
the bowl and mix until well combined.

lemon curd

3 egg yolks
finely grated zest of 1 lemon
60 ml (1/4 cup) lemon juice
115 g (1/2 cup) caster (superfine) sugar
50 g (1 3/4 oz) unsalted butter, cut into small pieces

Place the yolks, zest, juice and sugar in a heatproof bowl and whisk together until smooth.
Place the bowl over a saucepan of simmering water, making sure the bowl does not touch
the water. Stir for 8 to 10 minutes, or until thickened slightly. Remove from the heat and
whisk in the butter, one piece at a time, until smooth. Cool.

oat, pear and raspberry loaf

topping
25 g (1/4 cup) rolled oats
55 g (1/4 cup) brown sugar
2 tablespoons plain (all-purpose) flour
25 g (1 oz) chilled butter, cut into small pieces

cake
100 g (1 cup) rolled oats
375 ml (11/2 cups) boiling water
150 g (51/2 oz) unsalted butter, diced
115 g (1/2 cup) brown sugar
55 g (1/4 cup) caster (superfine) sugar
2 eggs
1 teaspoon natural vanilla extract
185 g (11/2 cups) plain (all-purpose) flour
a pinch of sea salt
1 teaspoon baking powder
2 ripe pears, peeled, cored and diced
60 g (1/2 cup) raspberries, fresh or frozen

to serve
butter

Preheat the oven to 180°C (350°F/Gas 4). To make the topping, place all the ingredients into a bowl and rub the butter into the mixture with your fingertips until well incorporated and small clumps form.

To make the cake, place the oats into a bowl and pour over the boiling water. Stir and leave to cool until lukewarm. Cream the butter and sugars in a bowl until pale and creamy. Add the eggs, one at a time, beating well after each addition. Mix in the vanilla. Sift the flour, salt and baking powder into the bowl. Drain any excess water off the oats. Add the oats to the mixture and fold to combine. Spread two-thirds of the mixture into a greased or non-stick 19 x 11 cm (71/2 x 41/2 inch) loaf tin. Sprinkle with the pears and raspberries, top with the remaining cake batter then sprinkle the topping over evenly.

Bake for 1 hour 10 minutes, or until a skewer inserted into the centre of the cake comes out clean. Turn out onto a plate before quickly transferring to a wire rack with the topping facing upwards. Leave to cool slightly before cutting. Serve in slices with butter. Makes 8 to 10 slices

mango lassi

125 g (1/2 cup) plain yoghurt
125 ml (1/2 cup) orange juice
1 mango, cubed
3 large ice cubes

Place all the ingredients in a blender and blend until the mango is well combined. Pour into a tall glass and serve. Makes 1

raspberry and strawberry smoothie

4 strawberries, hulled
30 g (1/4 cup) raspberries
15 g (1/2 oz) plain yoghurt
125 ml (1/2 cup) milk
3–4 large ice cubes

Place all the ingredients in a blender and blend until smooth. Pour into a tall glass and serve. Makes 1

lunch

lunch

'It's funny, but things always seem to taste better when you travel. And I don't just mean from country to country. Just going to have dim sum on the other side of town makes the whole experience quite different and more memorable. There's something wonderful about the unexpected, and the sense of discovery. One of the best lunches I've had was a complete surprise, like most of my favourite meals. We were driving down the south coast of New South Wales when our car broke down in Tathra, a tiny seaside village. We discovered a tiny kiosk on a wharf that sat over the most beautiful bay. I'll never forget the plate of fresh prawns and simple mayonnaise I had that day. Not surprisingly, my idea of a perfect dining room is anywhere outdoors, with a chorus of cicadas in the background and the scent of frangipani flowers wafting on the air. Such a perfect setting doesn't need much embellishment—just keep the food as simple and as fresh as possible.'

I like to serve my fried rice with a dish of chopped
red chillies in fish sauce on the side.

thai fried rice

2 tablespoons canola, or a light-flavoured oil

3 garlic cloves, crushed (I do this in a mortar and pestle with a small pinch of salt)

370 g (2 cups) cold cooked rice, preferably jasmine

1/2 small red onion, sliced

1/2 tomato, cut into three wedges

30 g (1/2 cup) finely sliced green vegetables such as snow peas (mangetout), broccolini or
    Chinese broccoli

1 egg, lightly beaten, optional

1 tablespoon fish sauce

to serve
coriander (cilantro) sprigs

1/2 Lebanese (short) cucumber, sliced

1 lime cheek

Heat a wok or a non-stick frying pan over a high heat until hot. Put the oil in and swirl to
coat the base of the pan. Stir-fry the garlic for 1 minute, then add the rice and stir for
2 minutes. Add the onion, tomato and green vegetables and stir-fry for another minute.
Make a well in the centre of the rice and pour in the egg, if using. Lightly scramble for
20 seconds until nearly cooked, then fold through the rest of the rice. Sprinkle with the fish
sauce and stir to combine. Serve with the coriander sprigs, cucumber slices and a lime cheek.

Serves 1 as you should cook each portion separately. I have all the ingredients ready so
I can quickly prepare the next serve.

Lentils du Puy are green lentils from Le Puy in France. I think they are particularly good because they are quick to cook and maintain their shape during cooking. If you can't find them, use regular brown or green lentils instead.

honey lemon chicken wings with lentil feta salad

16 free-range chicken wings, tips removed
   and jointed
1 1/2 teaspoons sea salt
125 ml (1/2 cup) lemon juice
5 garlic cloves, crushed
90 g (1/4 cup) honey

to serve
flat-leaf (Italian) parsley, to garnish
lentil feta salad (below)
lemon wedges

Preheat the oven to 200°C (400°F/Gas 6). Place the chicken wings in a baking dish, sprinkle with the salt then roast for 30 minutes. Place the lemon juice, garlic and honey in a small bowl and stir until the honey has dissolved. Pour over the chicken wings and stir until well coated. Cook for another 20 minutes. Garnish with parsley and serve with the lentil feta salad and lemon wedges. Serves 4

lentil feta salad

185 g (1 cup) lentils du Puy
3 tablespoons extra virgin olive oil
2 tablespoons lemon juice
sea salt
freshly ground black pepper
15 g (1/2 cup) shredded flat-leaf (Italian)
   parsley

12 fresh mint leaves
1/2 red onion, finely sliced
1 Lebanese (short) cucumber, sliced into
   four lengthways and diced
100 g (3 1/2 oz) feta cheese,
   crumbled

Place the lentils in a saucepan with 375 ml (1 1/2 cups) of water and bring to the boil. Reduce the heat and simmer for 15 to 20 minutes, or until tender. Strain and set aside. Place the olive oil, lemon juice, salt and pepper into a bowl and whisk until combined. Add the lentils and allow to cool. Add the parsley, mint, onion and cucumber and stir gently to combine. Place in a serving dish and top with the crumbled feta.

spicy omelette sandwiches

4 eggs
a large pinch of cumin
1 teaspoon extra virgin olive oil
sea salt
freshly ground black pepper

to serve
2 soft bap rolls
tomato salsa (below)

Break the eggs into a bowl. Add a tablespoon of water and the cumin. Beat lightly with a fork until just combined.

Heat a non-stick frying pan over a medium to high heat, add the oil and swirl to coat the base of the pan. Pour in the egg mixture and, as the mixture begins to cook, use a wooden spoon to carefully drag the cooked egg to the centre, allowing the uncooked mixture to flow towards the edges. Repeat a second time—this will only take a minute. Sprinkle with salt and pepper. When the omelette is nearly cooked, fold in half and slide out onto a board before cutting in half, lengthways. Split a bap roll in half, butter if desired, and fill with half an omelette and tomato salsa. Repeat with remaining ingredients. Serves 2

tomato salsa

3 tomatoes, seeded and cut in thin strips
1/2 red onion, finely sliced
15 g (1/4 cup) coriander (cilantro) leaves
1 tablespoon lime juice

1 tablespoon olive oil
1/2 long green chilli, finely sliced
sea salt
freshly ground black pepper

Place all the ingredients in a bowl and stir to combine.

I find the quickest and easiest way to make thin zucchini ribbons is to use a vegetable peeler.

spiced zucchini soup

2 small white onions, or 1 large white onion, roughly sliced
1 tablespoon olive oil
sea salt
1 tablespoon curry powder
1 kg (2 lb 4 oz) zucchini (courgettes), sliced
1.5 litres (6 cups) vegetable or chicken stock
freshly ground black pepper
45 g (1/4 cup) white short-grain rice

to serve
plain yoghurt
1 zucchini (courgette), shaved into thin ribbons and lightly blanched

Place the onion, olive oil and salt in a large saucepan over a medium to high heat and cook for 5 minutes, or until the onion is translucent. Add the curry powder and cook for 2 minutes. Add the zucchini, stock, pepper and rice and bring to the boil. Reduce the heat to low and cook for another 20 minutes.

Blend the soup in a blender or food processor until smooth. Serve immediately with a dollop of yoghurt and garnish with zucchini ribbons. Serves 4

grilled tuna with sweet and spicy red capsicums

2 tablespoons olive oil
1 red onion, halved and finely sliced
2 red capsicums (peppers), cut into 1 cm (1/2 inch) strips
1 garlic clove, sliced
1 tomato, chopped
2 teaspoons caster (superfine) sugar
1/2–1 teaspoon chilli flakes
sea salt
freshly ground black pepper
1 tablespoon balsamic vinegar
2 tablespoons olive oil, extra
4 x 150 g (51/2 oz) tuna steaks

to serve
lemon wedges
flat-leaf (Italian) parsley, to garnish

Place a large saucepan over a medium heat and add the oil. Add the onion, capsicum and garlic and cook for about 5 minutes, or until softened. Reduce the heat, cover with a lid and cook for 15 minutes.

Add 60 ml (1/4 cup) water, tomato, sugar, chilli, salt and pepper to the pan. Increase the heat to medium and cook for another 15 minutes uncovered. Remove from the heat and stir through the balsamic vinegar.

Heat a frying pan over a high heat until hot and add the extra oil. Cook the tuna for 1 minute on each side, or until cooked to your liking. Serve with the capsicum and lemon wedges and garnish with parsley. Serves 4

Tuna is a good fish to serve rare—I like to just sear each side.

This rice salad can be made ahead of time and refrigerated.
Just return to room temperature before serving.

prawn skewers with rice salad

3 thick slices sourdough or wholemeal
    bread, crusts removed
80 ml (1/3 cup) extra virgin olive oil
24 medium green prawns (shrimp), peeled
    and deveined
2 garlic cloves, crushed
7 g (1/4 cup) finely chopped flat-leaf
    (Italian) parsley

finely grated zest of 1 lemon
1 teaspoon sea salt
freshly ground black pepper

to serve
lemon wedges
rice salad (below)

Soak eight wooden skewers in water for 30 minutes to stop them from burning during cooking. Preheat the oven to 200°C (400°F/Gas 6). Place the bread on a baking tray and toast for 20 minutes, or until lightly golden. Remove from the oven and leave to cool. Crumble the toasted bread with your hands or process in a food processor until breadcrumbs form.

Place the olive oil and prawns in a large bowl and toss to combine. Add the remaining ingredients and stir thoroughly so that each prawn is evenly coated with breadcrumbs. Cover with plastic wrap and refrigerate for 30 minutes. Preheat a grill to high. Thread 3 prawns on each skewer, curling and skewering the tails to maintain a round shape. Place on a baking tray and cook for 2 minutes each side, or until golden. Serve with lemon wedges and the rice salad. Serves 4

rice salad

60 ml (1/4 cup) olive oil
2 tablespoons lemon juice
sea salt
freshly ground black pepper
740 g (4 cups) cooked short-grain white rice
1 tablespoon lemon zest

1/2 red onion, finely diced
l0 g (1/3 cup) roughly chopped flat-leaf
    (Italian) parsley
2 celery sticks, finely diced
75 g (1/3 cup) green olives, pitted and
    sliced

Combine the oil, lemon juice, salt and pepper in a serving bowl. Add the remaining ingredients and toss until well combined.

Sumac is a Middle Eastern spice made from the crimson berries of the sumac tree.

grilled chicken with chickpea salad

4 x 200 g (7 oz) chicken breasts
2 tablespoons olive oil
sea salt
freshly ground black pepper
250 g (1 cup) plain yoghurt
1 tablespoon lemon juice

to serve
chickpea salad (below)
sumac, to garnish
flat-leaf (Italian) parsley leaves, to garnish

Preheat the oven to 220°C (425°F/Gas 7). Heat a frying pan over a high heat and, while the pan is heating, brush the chicken with olive oil and season with salt and pepper. Place the chicken skin-side down and sear for 2 minutes, turn and sear for another minute. Transfer to a baking tray and cook in the oven for 8 to 10 minutes. Leave to rest for a couple of minutes. Meanwhile, place the yoghurt and lemon juice in a bowl and stir to combine. Season to taste. Divide the chickpea salad evenly onto four individual serving dishes. Slice the chicken breasts on the diagonal and place on top of the salad. Spoon over the yoghurt dressing and sprinkle with the sumac. Garnish with parsley. Serves 4

chickpea salad

2 x 400 g (14 oz) cans chickpeas, drained
3 tomatoes, cut into eighths
4 radishes, finely sliced
1/2 red onion, finely sliced
1 teaspoon sumac, optional

2 tablespoons olive oil
2 tablespoons lemon juice

Place all the ingredients in a bowl and toss to combine.

This salad is lovely served with a simple lemonade made from the juice of 1 lemon, 1 teaspoon of sugar and sparkling mineral water.

vietnamese chicken salad

3 x 200 g (7 oz) chicken breasts
2 tablespoons vegetable oil
sea salt
pepper (I like white pepper in this salad, but use black if that is all you have)
90 g (1 cup) bean sprouts
20 g (1 cup) Vietnamese mint leaves

50 g (1 cup) Asian basil leaves, or basil leaves
180 g (4 cups) Chinese cabbage, finely shredded
Vietnamese dressing (below)
90 g (1 cup) pickled carrot (below), or raw carrot, peeled and finely julienned

Preheat the oven to 220°C (425°F/Gas 7). Heat a frying pan over a high heat, and while the pan is heating, brush the chicken with olive oil and season with salt and pepper. Place the chicken skin-side down and sear for 2 minutes, turn and sear for another minute. Put the chicken on a baking tray and cook in the oven for 8 to 10 minutes. Leave to rest for 20 minutes. Shred the chicken into thin strips with your hands and place in a large bowl. Add the remaining ingredients and toss to combine. Serves 4

vietnamese dressing

60 ml (1/4 cup) lime juice
60 ml (1/4 cup) fish sauce
2 tablespoons rice vinegar
1 tablespoon caster (superfine) sugar
2 garlic cloves, very finely chopped

3 red Asian shallots, or 1/2 red onion, finely sliced
2 small red chillies, very finely chopped (and seeds removed, if you don't like the heat)

Place all the ingredients in a small bowl and stir until the sugar is dissolved.

pickled carrot

250 g (9 oz) carrots, peeled and finely julienned
1 teaspoon sea salt

2 tablespoons rice vinegar
1 tablespoon caster (superfine) sugar

Place the carrots in a colander, sprinkle with salt and toss to combine. Leave for 20 minutes. While the carrot is resting, place 185 ml (3/4 cup) water with the vinegar and sugar in a small saucepan over a medium heat and bring to the boil. Remove from the heat and cool. Rinse the carrot, squeezing out any excess water, and place in a bowl. Pour over the pickling liquid and stand for 1 hour. Strain before serving.

Pomelo is a large citrus fruit that is roughly the size of two grapefruits. It tastes similar to a sweet grapefruit, and its drier texture makes it ideal for salads. You will find them in Asian food stores.

grapefruit and prawn salad

2 ruby grapefruit or 2 grapefruit or
   1 pomelo
40 g (1/4 cup) cashews
20 cooked prawns (shrimp), peeled and
   deveined
20 g (1 cup) mint leaves

1 small butter lettuce, washed and dried
dressing (below)

to serve
steamed rice

Peel the grapefruit by slicing off both ends. Stand the end of the fruit on a board, and following the curves of the grapefruit, slice off all the peel with a sharp knife. Make sure the pith is also removed. Slice out segments of the grapefruit by cutting in between the membrane. Set aside. Place a frying pan over a high heat and when hot, add the cashews. Cook, stirring for 2 to 3 minutes, or until lightly roasted. Remove from the heat and roughly chop. Set aside.

Place the grapefruit, prawns and mint in a bowl. Add the dressing and toss to combine. Arrange the lettuce leaves on a large serving plate, or divide between four plates. Top with the salad and sprinkle with the roasted cashews. Serve with steamed rice. Serves 4

dressing

60 ml (1/4 cup) fish sauce
60 ml (1/4 cup) lime juice
2 tablespoons brown sugar

3 red Asian shallots, or 1/2 red onion,
   finely sliced
2 small red chillies, finely chopped

Place all the ingredients in a small bowl and stir until the sugar is dissolved.

warm tomato and ricotta pasta salad

500 g (2 punnets) cherry tomatoes, cut in half
80 ml (1/3 cup) extra virgin olive oil
60 ml (1/4 cup) red wine vinegar
1/2 teaspoon caster (superfine) sugar
1 teaspoon sea salt
freshly ground black pepper
4 thick slices wholemeal or sourdough bread
1 garlic clove, sliced in half
2 tablespoons extra virgin olive oil, extra
500 g (1 lb 2 oz) rigatoni
60 g (1 cup) finely shredded basil leaves
250 g (9 oz) fresh ricotta cheese

Preheat the oven to 200°C (400°F/Gas 6). Place the tomatoes, olive oil, vinegar and sugar in a large bowl and stir to combine. Season with salt and pepper. Cover and leave to marinate while you prepare the rest of the dish.

Rub the bread on both sides with the cut side of the garlic. Brush with the extra olive oil and sprinkle with salt. Put the bread on a baking tray and place in the oven. Cook for 20 minutes, or until crisp. Remove from the oven and crumble into coarse breadcrumbs with your hands. Set aside.

Cook the pasta in a large pot of rapidly boiling salted water until *al dente*. Drain well, then add to the tomatoes. Add the basil and toss to combine.

Divide the pasta between four serving plates, or put it on one large serving dish, crumble over the ricotta cheese and sprinkle with the breadcrumbs. Serves 4

spaghetti with prosciutto and egg

500 g (1 lb 2 oz) spaghetti
60 ml (1/4 cup) extra virgin olive oil
2 garlic cloves, finely sliced
sea salt
8 slices prosciutto, chopped
60 ml (1/4 cup) white wine
4 eggs
35 g (1/3 cup) grated Parmesan cheese
60 g (1/2 cup) finely chopped spring onions (scallions)
freshly ground black pepper
shredded Parmesan cheese, extra

Cook the pasta in a large pot of rapidly boiling salted water until *al dente*. While the spaghetti is cooking, place a frying pan over a medium to high heat. Add the olive oil, garlic and a sprinkle of salt and cook, stirring, for 10 seconds. Add the prosciutto and cook for 2 minutes, stirring occasionally. Add the wine and cook for another minute. Remove from the heat. Place the eggs, cheese and spring onions in a large bowl and whisk with a fork until combined. Season with pepper. Combine the drained spaghetti with the prosciutto mixture, then add the egg mixture and toss to combine. The heat of the pasta will gently cook the egg. Divide between four bowls and top with the extra Parmesan cheese. Serves 4

As a general rule, the smaller the chilli, the hotter it is, but I always taste a seed just to double-check. Have a glass of water ready!

citrus risotto with garlic chilli prawns

1.5 litres (6 cups) chicken stock
1 tablespoon olive oil
1 small brown onion, finely diced
1 teaspoon sea salt
50 g (1 3/4 oz) butter
330 g (1 1/2 cups) arborio rice
finely grated zest of 1 lemon
1 tablespoon lemon juice
freshly ground black pepper
2 small red chillies
2 garlic cloves
2 tablespoons olive oil, extra
20 green prawns (shrimp), shelled with tails intact, and deveined

to serve
7 g (1/4 cup) roughly chopped flat-leaf (Italian) parsley
lemon wedges

Place the stock in a large saucepan and bring to the boil over a high heat. Reduce the heat and keep at simmering point. Place a large heavy-based saucepan over a medium heat and add the olive oil, onion, salt and half the butter. Stir until the onion is translucent. Add the rice and stir for 1 to 2 minutes, or until the rice is well coated.

Gradually add all the simmering stock, a cupful at a time, stirring constantly and making sure the stock is absorbed before you add more. This should take 20 minutes and the rice should be *al dente* and creamy. Remove the saucepan from the heat, then stir in the remaining butter, lemon zest, lemon juice and pepper to taste. Cover the saucepan and leave to sit for 3 minutes for the flavours to develop.

Meanwhile, pound the chilli and garlic in a mortar and pestle. Place the extra olive oil in a frying pan over a high heat and heat until hot. Season the prawns with salt and pepper. Cook for 2 minutes, shaking the pan, until the prawns are just opaque then add the chilli and garlic and cook for 1 minute. Remove from the heat and set aside.

Stir the risotto and divide between four bowls. Toss the prawns with the parsley then place on top of the risotto. Serve with lemon wedges. Serves 4

snapper fillet with asparagus salad and soy dressing

4 x 180 g (6^1/$_2$ oz) snapper fillets, skin on
sea salt
freshly ground black pepper
1 tablespoon vegetable oil
310 g (2 bunches) asparagus, cut into thirds
   on the diagonal and blanched
1 telegraph (long) cucumber, shaved into
   thin strips

1 large red chilli, seeded and sliced finely
   on the diagonal
10 g (^{1}/$_2$ cup) mint leaves
25 g (^{3}/$_4$ cup) coriander (cilantro) leaves

to serve
soy dressing (below)

Using a sharp knife, cut three slashes into the skin side of the fish and season with salt and
pepper. Place a non-stick frying pan over a high heat and add the oil. Place the fish skin-side
down in the pan and cook for 3 minutes. Turn and cook on the other side for 2 to 3 minutes,
or until the fish is opaque and just cooked. Place the asparagus, cucumber, chilli, mint and
coriander in a bowl and toss to combine. Serve the fish with the salad and drizzle with the
soy dressing. Serves 4

soy dressing

2 tablespoons soy sauce
2 tablespoons fish sauce
60 ml (^{1}/$_4$ cup) lime juice
2 tablespoons caster (superfine) sugar

1 small red chilli, julienned
3 red Asian shallots, or ^{1}/$_2$ small red onion,
   finely sliced

Place all the ingredients in a bowl and mix to combine.

Brown or yellow onions are best for cooking with as they have a stronger flavour than the sweeter red or white onions which are better in salads.

briget's onion and feta cheese tart

2 tablespoons olive oil
1 kg (2 lb 4 oz) onions, finely sliced
1 tablespoon soft brown sugar
2 tablespoons balsamic vinegar
1 teaspoon sea salt
freshly ground black pepper
1 x 375 g (13 oz) packet puff pastry
25 g (1/2 cup) finely grated Parmesan cheese
150 g (51/2 oz) feta cheese, crumbled
2 tablespoons oregano leaves

Place the olive oil and onion in a saucepan over a medium heat and cook for 20 minutes, stirring occasionally. Add the sugar, balsamic vinegar, salt and pepper. Cook for another 5 minutes, or until the onion is soft and caramelized. Remove from the heat and set aside to cool.

Meanwhile, preheat the oven to 220°C (425°F/Gas 7). Roll out the pastry to a 20 x 40 cm (8 x 16 inches) rectangle on a lightly floured surface. Trim the edges with a sharp knife and place on a lined baking tray. Score a 1 cm (1/4 inch) border around the edge of the pastry, taking care not to cut all the way through to the bottom. Prick the pastry with a fork and sprinkle the Parmesan cheese within the scored edges.

Place the onion on top of the pastry base. Bake in the oven for 20 to 25 minutes, or until the pastry is puffed and golden brown. Remove from the oven and sprinkle with the feta cheese and oregano leaves. Serves 6

open-faced chicken sandwiches

2 x 200 g (7 oz) skinless chicken breasts
1 tablespoon olive oil
sea salt
freshly ground black pepper
125 g (1/2 cup) good-quality mayonnaise
1 tablespoon lime juice
4 spring onions (scallions), finely sliced
2 tablespoons chopped flat-leaf (Italian) parsley
finely grated zest of 1 lime
4 slices good-quality brown bread
1 Lebanese (short) cucumber, peeled into ribbons
15 g (1/2 cup) coriander (cilantro) leaves
1/2 iceberg lettuce, cut into 4 wedges

Preheat the oven to 220°C (425°F/Gas 7). Place the chicken breasts on a baking tray, brush with olive oil and season with salt and pepper. Place the chicken in the oven and cook for 10 to 12 minutes. Remove from the oven, cover with foil and allow to rest for 15 minutes. Slice the chicken lengthways into 5 mm (1/4 inch) slices.

Place the mayonnaise, lime juice, a little salt and pepper, spring onion, parsley and zest in a bowl and stir to combine.

Spread each slice of bread with some of the mayonnaise mixture. Top with the chicken, cucumber and coriander. Serve with a wedge of lettuce. Makes 4

I like to use fresh spinach pasta, but plain egg
noodles will be just as delicious.

tagliatelle with chicken and green beans

2 x 200 g (7 oz) chicken breasts, thinly sliced
2 tablespoons extra virgin olive oil
3 garlic cloves, finely sliced
sea salt
freshly ground black pepper
375 g (13 oz) tagliatelle
2 tablespoons olive oil
200 g (7 oz) baby green beans, topped (not tailed) and sliced from end to end
   on the diagonal
125 ml (1/2 cup) chicken stock
good-quality Parmesan cheese, grated
50 g (1/4 cup) basil leaves

Place the chicken, extra virgin olive oil and garlic in a bowl and stir to combine. Season with
salt and pepper. Cook the pasta in a large pot of rapidly boiling salted water until *al dente*
and drain well. Meanwhile, 5 minutes before the pasta is cooked, place a large frying pan
over a high heat until hot. Add the extra olive oil and heat for 5 seconds. Add the chicken
with the marinade and sear quickly for 30 seconds. Add the beans and reduce the heat to
medium. Cook for another 2 minutes, stirring occasionally. Return the heat to high, add the
stock and simmer for 30 seconds. Add the pasta and toss to combine.

Divide the pasta evenly between four bowls and top with freshly grated Parmesan cheese,
basil and lots of freshly ground black pepper. Serves 4

I find that squeezing lemon over haloumi really brings out the flavour.

greek salad with pan-fried haloumi

2 tablespoons extra virgin olive oil

2 tablespoons lemon juice

sea salt

freshly ground black pepper

4 ripe tomatoes, halved and cut into thirds

2 Lebanese (short) cucumbers, quartered lengthways and cut into chunks

1 red onion, finely sliced

20 g (1 cup) mint leaves

20 g (1 cup) flat-leaf (Italian) parsley leaves

95 g (1/2 cup) Kalamata, or other black olives

1 tablespoon olive oil

250 g (9 oz) haloumi cheese, cut lengthways into 1 cm (1/2 inch) slices

Place the extra virgin olive oil and lemon juice in a bowl and mix to combine. Season with salt and pepper. Add the tomato, cucumber, onion, mint, parsley and olives. Toss until the salad is evenly coated with the dressing.

Place a large frying pan over a medium to high heat and add the olive oil. Cook the haloumi slices for 1 minute on each side, or until golden. Remove and place on paper towels to drain. Divide the salad among four serving plates and top with the haloumi slices. Serves 4

I buy my roast ducks in Chinatown at a Chinese barbecue shop.

barbecued duck salad

1 Chinese roast duck
6 spring onions (scallions), sliced on the diagonal
2 Lebanese (short) cucumbers, julienned
30 g (1 cup) coriander (cilantro) leaves
1 large red chilli, finely sliced

to serve
dressing (below)
steamed rice

Pull the skin and meat from the duck with your fingers, roughly shredding the skin. Place the duck, spring onion, cucumber, coriander and chilli in a bowl and toss to combine. Drizzle over the dressing just before serving with steamed rice, or serve alongside. Serves 4

dressing

$2^1/_2$ tablespoons hoisin sauce
2 tablespoons soy sauce

1 tablespoon balsamic vinegar
2 teaspoons sesame oil

Place all the ingredients in a bowl and stir to combine.

A nice alternative is to make a simple herb crust
by mixing chopped parsley and coriander together with chilli,
lemon zest, salt, pepper and olive oil. Press firmly on the fish,
refrigerate for 30 minutes then cook as below.

pan-fried fish with lemon potato salad

olive oil, for greasing the pan
4 x 200 g (7 oz) firm white fish fillets such as
   snapper, skin removed

to serve
lemon wedges
mint leaves, to garnish
lemon potato salad (below)

Heat a little oil in a large non-stick frying pan over a medium to high heat until hot. Add
the fish and cook for 3 minutes. Turn and cook on the other side for 2 to 3 minutes, or until
the fish is opaque and just cooked. Garnish with mint leaves and serve with lemon wedges
and the lemon potato salad. Serves 4

lemon potato salad

750 g (1 lb 10 oz) waxy potatoes, such as
   kipfler, peeled and sliced
1 teaspoon sea salt
80 ml (1/3 cup) extra virgin olive oil
125 ml (1/2 cup) lemon juice
1 teaspoon sumac, optional
sea salt, extra

freshly ground black pepper
1 small green capsicum (pepper), finely diced
2 large red chillies, seeded and finely diced
15 g (1/4 cup) chopped mint
30 g (1/2 cups) flat-leaf (Italian) parsley
   leaves
6 spring onions (scallions), finely sliced

Bring a large pot of water to the boil over a high heat. Add the potatoes and salt, reduce
the heat to medium and simmer for about 8 to 10 minutes until the potatoes are tender
when pierced with a knife. Remember to undercook the potatoes a little, because they will
continue cooking when removed from the water.

Place the olive oil, lemon juice and sumac in a bowl and stir to combine. Season with salt
and pepper. Pour half the dressing over the hot potatoes and stir gently. Leave to cool.
Add the capsicum, chilli, mint, parsley, spring onion and remaining dressing and stir gently.

spicy squid salad

1 baby cos lettuce, washed and dried
1 kg (2 lb 4 oz) squid, cleaned, scored on
  inside and cut into strips
2 tablespoons vegetable oil
3 red Asian shallots, or 1/2 red onion,
  finely sliced
20 g (1 cup) mint leaves

30 g (1 cup) coriander (cilantro) sprigs
50 g (1 cup) Asian basil leaves, or basil leaves
2 long red chillies, seeded and very
  finely sliced

to serve
chilli garlic dressing (below)

Arrange the lettuce leaves on four serving plates. Place the squid and vegetable oil in a bowl and toss to combine. Preheat a barbecue or frying pan until hot. Cook the squid for 1 to 2 minutes each side, or until just cooked. Don't overcook or the squid will be tough.

Place the onion, mint, coriander, basil and chilli in a bowl with the cooked squid. Pour the chilli garlic dressing over and toss to combine. Pile on top of the lettuce leaves. Serves 4

chilli garlic dressing

2 garlic cloves
1 small red chilli, roughly chopped
2 coriander (cilantro) roots, washed and
  scraped

1 teaspoon sea salt
55 g (1/4 cup) soft brown sugar
60 ml (1/4 cup) lime juice
60 ml (1/4 cup) fish sauce

Place the garlic, chilli, coriander root and salt in a mortar and pestle and pound into a paste. Add the sugar, lime juice and fish sauce and stir to combine. Alternatively, process in a food processor or blender until smooth.

afternoon tea

afternoon tea

'I want my family to grow up with good memories around food. A freshly brewed cup of tea with a slice of cake still warm from the oven or a tart made from freshly picked apricots will become part of a happy memory. In fact, nothing makes me feel happier than filling the house with the warm aroma of freshly baked cakes. Like many a budding cook, I tackled baking first when I started experimenting in the kitchen as a child and today I still feel a little of that seven-year-old boy's wonder. I can't wait until Edie is old enough to learn to make some of my recipes. She loves watching me cook and is at the shelling peas stage now, but I know she's not too far away from making a chocolate cake. A two-year-old's delight can be very inspiring.'

vanilla cup cakes

125 g (4¹/2 oz) unsalted butter, softened
250 g (1 cup) caster (superfine) sugar
1¹/2 teaspoons natural vanilla extract
3 eggs
185 g (1¹/2 cups) plain (all-purpose) flour

1 teaspoon baking powder
185 ml (³/4 cup) milk
icing (below)
fresh raspberries, to decorate

Preheat the oven to 180°C (350°F/Gas 4). Line a 12-hole 125 ml (¹/2 cup) muffin tray with paper cases. Place the butter and sugar in a bowl and beat until light and fluffy. Add the vanilla, then add the eggs, one at a time, beating well after each addition. Sift the flour, baking powder and ¹/2 teaspoon of salt and fold into the mixture, alternating with the milk, until it has a soft dropping consistency. Spoon into the cases and bake for 20–25 minutes until golden. Remove from the oven and cool for 10 minutes in the tin. Turn the cakes out onto a wire rack to cool. Ice the cakes when cold and top with raspberries. Makes 12

icing

60 g (¹/2 cup) icing (confectioners') sugar,
    sifted

2–3 teaspoons hot water
a few drops of natural vanilla extract

Place all the ingredients in a bowl and mix until smooth.

If fresh apricots are out of season, you can use bottled or canned ones.

apricot slice

185 g (1^1/$_2$ cups) plain (all-purpose) flour
170 g (^{3}/4 cup) caster (superfine) sugar
1 teaspoon baking powder
a pinch of salt
3 eggs
60 ml (^{1}/4 cup) milk
2 teaspoons natural vanilla extract
180 g (6^1/2 oz) butter, softened
14 apricots, pitted and halved (this may vary depending on the size of the apricots)
2 tablespoons caster (superfine) sugar, extra

Preheat the oven to 160°C (315°F/Gas 2–3). Sift the flour, sugar, baking powder and salt into a large bowl and make a well in the centre. Place the eggs, milk and vanilla in another bowl and mix to combine. Pour the egg mixture and butter into the well in the dry ingredients and beat for 2 minutes until smooth. Spread the mixture evenly into a greased or non-stick 20 x 30 cm (8 x 12 inch) lamington tin.

Push the apricot halves, cut side up, evenly into the cake mixture in four rows of seven. Place in the oven and bake for 20 minutes, sprinkle over extra sugar and cook for another 20 minutes, or until a skewer inserted into the centre comes out clean.

Cut into fingers with two apricot halves per slice. Makes 14 slices

coconut and lime macadamia cake

200 g (7 oz) macadamia nuts
40 g (1/3 cup) self-raising flour
a pinch of salt
6 eggs, separated
165 g (3/4 cup) sugar

finely grated zest of 1 lime
45 g (1/2 cup) desiccated coconut
lime icing (below)

Preheat the oven to 180°C (350°F/Gas 4). Place the nuts, flour and salt in the bowl of a food processor and process until the nuts are ground. Place the egg yolks and sugar in a bowl and beat for 3 minutes, or until the mixture is pale and creamy. Fold through the zest and coconut then the nut mixture. Place the egg whites in a clean, dry stainless steel bowl and whisk until stiff peaks form. Using a large metal spoon, fold lightly through the nut batter.

Spread the batter evenly into a 23 cm (9 inch) greased or non-stick springform cake tin. Bake for 40 minutes, or until the cake is lightly golden.

Remove from the oven and leave to sit for 10 minutes in the tin. Turn the cake out onto a serving plate. Spread the lime icing over the warm cake, allowing it to drizzle down the sides.

lime icing

125 g (1 cup) icing (confectioners') sugar, sifted

2 tablespoons lime juice
1 teaspoon finely grated lime zest

Combine all the ingredients in a bowl and mix until smooth and glossy.

honey cheesecake

60 g (¹/2 cup) sultanas
60 ml (¹/4 cup) Marsala, or cold weak tea
55 g (¹/4 cup) caster (superfine) sugar
6 large eggs
finely grated zest of 1 orange
90 g (¹/4 cup) honey
1 kg (2 lb 4 oz) good-quality ricotta, lightly mashed to break up any lumps
icing (confectioners') sugar, for dusting

to serve
125 g (1 cup) raspberries

Preheat the oven to 160°C (315°F/Gas 2–3). Place the sultanas and Marsala in a small bowl and leave to soak for 30 minutes.

Place the sugar and eggs in a large bowl and beat for 5 minutes, or until light and foamy. Drain the sultanas then fold through the egg mixture with the zest, honey and ricotta until combined.

Pour the batter into a 23 cm (9 inch) greased or non-stick springform cake tin. Bake for 80 minutes, or until golden. The cake will wobble slightly in the centre.

Remove from the oven and leave to cool in the tin. Turn the cake out onto a serving platter, dust with icing sugar and serve with raspberries.

Because this cake is so simple, I love to use fresh ricotta cut from a wheel rather than from a tub. If you do find that your ricotta is watery, leave it to drain in a colander for 30 minutes before using.

Make sure you fill your pie well because the filling
will collapse a little during cooking.

peach and blackberry pie

1 kg (2 lb 4 oz) peaches, thickly sliced
150 g (1 cup) blackberries
1 tablespoon lemon juice
115 g (^{1}/2 cup) caster (superfine) sugar
1 teaspoon natural vanilla extract
2 tablespoons cornflour (cornstarch)

2 egg yolks, lightly beaten
2 tablespoons caster (superfine) sugar,
  extra

to serve
vanilla ice cream (optional)

Place the peaches, blackberries, lemon juice, sugar and vanilla in a large colander set over a
bowl to catch the liquid. Leave to sit for 2 hours, stirring occasionally. Pour the liquid into
a small saucepan over a high heat and bring to the boil. Cook for 3 to 5 minutes, until
reduced by about half and syrupy. Combine the cornflour with 1 tablespoon warm water in
a bowl then stir in the peach syrup until smooth. Put the peaches and blackberries into the
bowl, then stir in the peach syrup mixture.

Place half of the pastry on a lightly floured surface and roll out until 5 mm (^{1}/4 inches) thick.
Lightly press into a 23 cm (9 inch) pie tin. Spread the peach filling evenly inside the pie
shell. Roll out the remaining pastry on a lightly floured surface until 5 mm (^{1}/4 inches) thick.
Moisten the edges of the pie shell with the beaten egg yolk then cover pie with pastry.
Trim and press the edges firmly together, crimping with your fingertips. Using a sharp knife,
make several slashes on the top of the pie. Chill for 30 minutes. Preheat the oven to 200°C
(400°F/Gas 6). Place a baking tray in the oven and warm for 10 minutes. Brush the top of the
pie with the remaining egg yolk and sprinkle with the extra sugar. Place on the baking tray
and bake for 30 minutes. Lower the oven temperature to 180°C (350°F/Gas 4) and bake for
another 30 minutes, or until the crust is golden brown. If the crust starts to brown too quickly,
cover lightly with foil. Cool for 30 minutes before serving with vanilla ice cream, if desired.

shortcrust pastry

500 g (4 cups) plain (all-purpose) flour
60 g (^{1}/2 cup) icing (confectioners') sugar
a pinch of salt

360 g (12 oz) unsalted butter, chilled
  and cubed
125 g (^{1}/2 cup) sour cream

Place the flour, sifted sugar and salt in a bowl. Add the butter and rub through with your
fingertips, or place all the ingredients in the bowl of a food processor and process until
the mixture resembles coarse breadcrumbs. Add just enough sour cream for the dough
to come together in a ball. Divide the dough into two balls, wrap in plastic wrap and chill
for 30 minutes.

chocolate custard tarts

3 egg yolks
55 g (^{1}/4 cup) caster (superfine) sugar
2 tablespoons cornflour (cornstarch)
1 teaspoon natural vanilla extract
185 ml (^{3}/4 cup) cream
150 g (1 cup) dark chocolate, grated
2 sheets puff pastry
icing (confectioners') sugar, for dusting

Preheat the oven to 220°C (425°F/Gas 7). Place the egg yolks, sugar, cornflour and vanilla into a bowl and whisk until smooth. Add the cream and 125 ml (^{1}/2 cup) water and whisk again. Pour into a saucepan and place over a medium heat. Stir until the mixture is thick, about 5 minutes. Remove from the heat, add the chocolate and stir until melted. Leave to cool.

Place the sheets of puff pastry on top of each other and roll up. Cut into 1 cm (^{1}/2 inch) wide slices and roll out into rounds 10 cm (4 inches) in diameter. Lightly grease a non-stick 6-hole and a 12-hole 125 ml (^{1}/2 cup) muffin tin and push each round into the individual holes. Place in the freezer and chill for 10 minutes. Remove and divide the custard mixture evenly between the tart shells.

Place in the oven and bake for 20 minutes, or until the pastry is golden. Remove from the oven and leave to cool in the tins for 10 minutes before removing. Dust with icing sugar and serve. Makes 18

The most important thing to remember when melting chocolate is not to overheat it. If the temperature is too high, your chocolate will end up with a grainy texture.

mandarin chocolate cake

250 g (9 oz) good-quality dark chocolate, chopped into small pieces
250 g (9 oz) unsalted butter, chopped into small pieces
6 eggs, separated
115 g (1/2 cup) caster (superfine) sugar
3 tablespoons plain (all-purpose) flour, sifted
25 g (1/4 cup) almond meal
1 tablespoon mandarin zest (if mandarins are out of season, use oranges or tangerines)

to serve
cocoa, for dusting
mandarin slices
lightly whipped cream

Preheat the oven to 190°C (375°F/Gas 5). Place the chocolate and butter in a heatproof bowl over a saucepan of simmering water, making sure the bowl does not touch the water. Stir the chocolate and butter over the heat until just melted, being careful not to overheat. Remove from the heat and set aside.

Place the egg yolks and sugar in a bowl and mix until lightly combined. Gradually add the melted chocolate to the egg mixture, stirring constantly. Using a large metal spoon, fold through the flour, almond meal and mandarin zest.

Place the egg whites in a clean, dry stainless steel bowl and whisk until stiff peaks form. Using a large metal spoon, fold half of the egg whites lightly through the batter until barely combined. Fold through the remaining egg whites, again barely combining.

Pour the batter into a 23 cm (9 inch) greased or non-stick springform cake tin and bake for 35 minutes. Don't worry if the cake still seems to be very wet in the centre: it will firm up a little on cooling.

Remove the cake from the oven and leave to cool completely in the tin. Transfer to a serving platter and dust with cocoa. Serve with the mandarin slices and lightly whipped cream.

This recipe can also be made very successfully with Granny Smith apples. Cook the sliced apples in the caramel for 5 minutes before placing in the tin and topping with the cake mixture.

banana maple upside-down cake

50 g (1³/4 oz) unsalted butter plus 100 g (3¹/2 oz) unsalted butter, softened, extra
55 g (¹/4 cup) brown sugar
60 ml (¹/4 cup) maple syrup
3–4 bananas, sliced in half lengthways
230 g (1 cup) caster (superfine) sugar
4 eggs
1 teaspoon natural vanilla extract
155 g (1¹/4 cup) plain (all-purpose) flour
1 teaspoon baking powder
pinch of salt

to serve
vanilla ice cream (optional)

Preheat the oven to 180°C (350°F/Gas 4). To make the topping, place the butter, brown sugar and maple syrup in a small saucepan. Cook on a medium heat for 10 minutes, or until the sugar melts and the syrup is rich and golden. Pour the syrup into a 23 cm (9 inch) greased or non-stick springform cake tin and arrange the sliced bananas, cut-side down, over the base of the tin.

To make the cake, place the extra butter and caster sugar in a bowl and beat until pale and creamy. Add the eggs one at a time, beating after each addition, then add the vanilla. Sift the flour, baking powder and salt and gently fold through the mixture. Spoon the batter evenly over the bananas and caramel and smooth the top with a spatula.

Place the cake in the oven on a baking tray to catch any escaping caramel and bake for 35 minutes, or until a skewer inserted into the centre of the cake comes out clean.

Remove from the oven and leave in the tin for 5 minutes to cool slightly. Transfer to a large serving plate. Serve warm with vanilla ice cream, if desired.

pistachio biscuits

125 g (4¹/2 oz) shelled pistachios
125 g (4¹/2 oz) unsalted butter, softened
115 g (¹/2 cup) caster (superfine) sugar
1 egg
1 tablespoon rose-water

185 g (1¹/2 cups) plain (all-purpose) flour, sifted
1 teaspoon baking powder, sifted
2 tablespoons plain (all-purpose) flour, extra

Place the pistachios in a small bowl, cover with water and set aside for 30 minutes. (It is important to soak the pistachios so you can slice through them when cutting the dough.) Place the butter and sugar in a bowl and beat until pale and creamy. Add the egg and mix until combined. Add the rose-water, and stir until smooth. Drain the pistachios well then add to the batter with the flour and baking powder. Fold through until a stiff dough forms.

Sift the extra flour over a clean dry surface, and knead the dough lightly for 30 seconds. Divide the dough in half and roll each into a log, roughly 5 cm (2 inches) in diameter. Wrap each log in plastic wrap and refrigerate for 30 minutes.

Preheat the oven to 180°C (350°F/Gas 4). Remove the dough logs from the refrigerator, and slice into 5 mm (¹/4 inch) rounds. Place the biscuits 2 cm (³/4 inch) apart on a baking tray lined with baking paper. Place the biscuits in the oven and bake for 10 to 12 minutes, or until lightly golden. Remove from the oven and leave to cool on a wire rack. Makes 60

orange and cardamom biscuits

375 g (3 cups) plain (all-purpose) flour
2 teaspoons baking powder
1 tablespoon ground ginger
1 teaspoon ground nutmeg
1 teaspoon ground cardamom
250 g (9 oz) unsalted butter, softened

345 g (1¹/2 cups) brown sugar
3 teaspoons brandy
finely grated zest of 1 orange
30 g (¹/4 cup) plain (all-purpose) flour, extra
1 egg white, for glazing
30 g (¹/4 cup) granulated sugar

Sift the flour, baking powder, ginger, nutmeg and cardamom into a large bowl. Place the butter and brown sugar in a bowl and beat until pale and creamy. Add the brandy and zest and mix well. Using a large metal spoon, fold the dry ingredients through in two batches. Sift the extra flour over a clean dry surface and knead the dough for 30 seconds. Roll the dough into a large rectangle 5 mm (¹/4 inch) thick. Cut into shapes 3 x 6 cm (1¹/4 x 2¹/2 inches) long. Brush with the egg white and sprinkle with sugar.

Preheat the oven to 180°C (350°F/Gas 4). Place the biscuits 2 cm (³/4 inches) apart on a baking tray lined with baking paper. Bake for 10 to 12 minutes, or until lightly browned. Remove from the oven and leave to cool on a wire rack. Makes 40

baked lemon lime tart with fresh strawberry salad

4 eggs
170 g (3/4 cup) caster (superfine) sugar
125 ml (1/2 cup) cream
80 ml (1/3 cup) lemon juice
80 ml (1/3 cup) lime juice
baked sweet shortcrust pastry shell (below)
    or a ready-made shortcrust pastry shell

to serve
250 g (1 punnet) strawberries, hulled and
    cut into quarters
1 tablespoon honey
1 tablespoon Cointreau (optional)
thick (double/heavy) cream (optional)

Preheat the oven to 160°C (315°F/Gas 2–3). Place the eggs and sugar in a bowl and whisk to combine. Add the cream then the lemon and lime juices and whisk lightly until just combined. Pour the mixture into the cooled pastry shell and bake for 25 to 30 minutes, or until just set. Remove from the oven and leave to cool. Place the strawberries, honey and Cointreau, if using, into a bowl and toss gently to combine. Leave to sit for 20 minutes. Serve with the tart and double cream, if desired.

baked sweet shortcrust pastry shell

250 g (2 cups) plain (all-purpose) flour
125 g (1/4 cup) icing (confectioners') sugar,
    sifted
a pinch of salt

180 g (6 1/2 oz) unsalted butter, chilled and
    cubed
60 ml (1/4 cup) iced water

Place the flour, icing sugar and salt into a bowl and stir to combine. Using your fingertips, rub the butter through until the mixture resembles coarse breadcrumbs. Add the water and mix until the dough comes together in a ball. Shape into a round, wrap in plastic wrap and chill for 30 minutes. Roll out on a lightly floured surface until 3 mm (1/8 inch) thick. Press into a greased or non-stick 23 cm (9 inch) tart tin and prick pastry with a fork. Chill for 30 minutes.

Preheat the oven to 200°C (400°F/Gas 6). Line the chilled pastry with baking paper and add baking weights or rice. Bake for 15 minutes, then remove the paper and weights. Bake for another 10 minutes, or until golden and crisp. Leave to cool.

lemon lime meringue tart

6 egg whites
340 g (1 1/3 cup) caster (superfine) sugar

a pinch of cream of tartar

Place all the ingredients in a clean, dry stainless steel bowl and beat with electric mixers for 10 minutes, or until thick and glossy. Make the tart as above and cool completely before chilling for 1 hour. Pile the meringue high on the chilled tart. Fold two tea towels into half and place on top of each other on a baking tray, then sit the tart on top. Bake for 8 to 10 minutes at 200°C (400°F/Gas 6), or until lightly browned. See the picture on page 85.

dinner

dinner

'I love it when I'm invited to someone else's house for
dinner, but I don't get asked that often. I suspect people
are afraid of what I might think of their cooking. If only
they knew it's not the food that makes or breaks an
occasion. I once had a drinks party and planned to make
a lot of complicated canapés, which was far too ambitious.
After I did the shopping and cleaned the house I hardly
had time to prepare the food. Once the guests started
arriving, I gave up. In the end, we ordered takeaway pizza,
which I topped with freshly chopped parsley and olives.
Everyone loved it and I managed to enjoy the party.
Don't worry if you make mistakes—being a good cook
comes from learning how to fix them. Being a good host
is about enjoying yourself as well as entertaining others.'

Polenta is thick and sticky and needs to be stirred regularly so it doesn't catch on the base of the pan.

baked polenta with a simple tomato sauce

1 tablespoon sea salt
225 g (8 oz) instant polenta
1 tablespoon extra virgin olive oil
simple tomato sauce (below)
350 g (12 oz) fresh ricotta

25 g (¹/4 cup) finely grated Parmesan cheese
freshly ground black pepper

Put 1.5 litres (6 cups) water in a large saucepan over a high heat and bring to the boil. Add the salt and pour the polenta, constantly stirring with a wooden spoon, into the water in a steady stream. Reduce the heat to low, cover and cook for another 10 minutes, stirring regularly.

Lightly oil a 30 x 20 cm (12 x 8 inch) baking dish with half the olive oil. Pour the cooked polenta into the prepared dish and spread evenly. Leave to cool and firm in the baking dish then turn out onto a cutting board. Cut the polenta into 5 cm (2 inch) squares.

Preheat the oven to 200°C (400°F/Gas 6). Lightly grease a 20 x 25 cm (8 x 10 inch) gratin dish or four individual dishes with the remaining oil. Place the polenta squares in a single layer, slightly overlapping. Pour the simple tomato sauce evenly over the polenta. Sprinkle the ricotta and Parmesan cheese over the top. Season with pepper. Bake for 30 minutes, or until golden. Serves 4

simple tomato sauce

2 x 425 g (15 oz) tins chopped Italian
    tomatoes
2 tablespoons extra virgin olive oil
1 teaspoon sea salt

1 teaspoon sugar
freshly ground black pepper
2 garlic cloves, crushed

Place the tomatoes in a saucepan over a medium heat and cook for 15 minutes, stirring occasionally. Add the remaining ingredients, cook for 1 minute then remove from the heat.

If you don't have rice vinegar, just use extra lime juice to taste. What you are looking for is a balance of sweet, salty and sour.

rice paper rolls

marinade
1 stalk fresh lemon grass, white part only, roughly chopped
3 garlic cloves
1 small red chilli, seeded
60 ml (1/4 cup) fish sauce
1 tablespoon lime juice
2 tablespoons vegetable oil

200 g (7 oz) rice vermicelli
2 x 300 g (10 1/2 oz) large rump steaks

to serve
1 oak leaf lettuce, washed and dried
Asian basil
mint leaves
2 Lebanese (short) cucumbers, halved lengthways, then thinly sliced on diagonal
20 large round rice paper wrappers
Vietnamese dipping sauce (below)

Place all the marinade ingredients with 3 tablespoons of water in a food processor or blender and process until smooth. Put the steaks in a bowl and pour the marinade over. Cover with plastic wrap and place in the refrigerator to marinate for 2 hours. Place the rice vermicelli in a bowl and cover with boiling water. Soak for 6 to 7 minutes, then drain and place on a serving dish.

Place a large frying pan over a high heat until hot. Sear the steaks for 2 minutes on each side, by which time they will be done if you like rare steak. Continue cooking over a medium heat for 1 to 2 minutes on each side for medium and 2 to 3 minutes on each side for well done. Remove the steaks and allow to rest for 2 minutes in a warm place. Slice thinly and place on a serving dish.

To serve, arrange the lettuce, basil, mint and cucumber on a large platter and place on the table, alongside the steak, vermicelli, rice paper wrappers and dipping sauce. Place a large bowl of hot water on the table. To wrap the rolls, your guests should first soften the rice paper wrappers in hot water and shake off any excess water. Place the wrapper on a plate, top with a little vermicelli, beef, cucumber, basil and mint in the middle and roll up, tucking in the sides. Place each roll in a lettuce leaf and dip into sauce.

vietnamese dipping sauce

60 ml (1/4 cup) fish sauce
60 ml (1/4 cup) lime juice
2 tablespoons rice vinegar
1 tablespoon caster (superfine) sugar

1 garlic clove, finely chopped
1 large red chilli, seeded and finely chopped

Place all the ingredients in a bowl and stir until the sugar is dissolved.

I love to make miniature versions of
these fritters to serve with drinks.

seared scallops, carrot fritters and a yoghurt dressing

12 medium-sized scallops, intestinal tract
    removed
2 tablespoons olive oil
sea salt
freshly ground black pepper

to serve
carrot fritters (below)
yoghurt dressing (below)
watercress

Place the scallops in a bowl, add the olive oil, season with salt and pepper and stir to combine. Heat a non-stick frying pan over a medium to high heat and cook the scallops for 1 minute each side.

Place 3 carrot fritters on a plate, top with the watercress and scallops and drizzle with the yoghurt dressing. Season with pepper. Serves 4

carrot fritters

60 g (^{1}/2 cup) plain (all-purpose) flour
125 ml (^{1}/2 cup) soda water
1 egg, lightly beaten
^{1}/4 teaspoon ground cumin
^{1}/4 teaspoon ground coriander
^{1}/4 teaspoon turmeric
1 teaspoon caster (superfine) sugar

1 teaspoon sea salt
1 small red chilli, seeded and finely chopped
235 g (1^1/2 cups) grated carrot
8 spring onions (scallions), finely sliced
25 g (^{1}/2 cup) chopped coriander (cilantro)
60 ml (^{1}/4 cup) vegetable oil

Preheat the oven to 160°C (315°F/Gas 2–3). Place the flour, soda water, egg, cumin, coriander, turmeric, sugar and salt in a bowl and mix well. Add the chilli, carrot, spring onion and coriander and stir to combine. Heat a frying pan on a medium to high heat, add the oil and heat until hot. Cooking in batches, add 2 tablespoons of batter per fritter and cook for 2 minutes each side, or until golden brown. Drain on paper towels. Cook the remaining fritter batter, adding extra oil if necessary. Place the fritters on an ovenproof plate lined with paper towels and keep warm in the oven while you cook the scallops.

yoghurt dressing

125 g (^{1}/2 cup) plain yoghurt
1 tablespoon lime juice
sea salt

freshly ground black pepper
1 tablespoon olive oil

Place all the ingredients in a bowl and whisk to combine.

To prepare mussels, I scrub them under running water with a clean kitchen scourer which works marvellously to remove any residual seaweed or slime. Discard any with broken shells and ones that don't close when tapped lightly on the bench.

stir-fried mussels with chilli and blackbean

2 teaspoons sugar
2 tablespoons soy sauce
3 tablespoons Shaoxing rice wine, or dry sherry
2 tablespoons vegetable oil
3 tablespoons finely sliced fresh ginger
4 spring onions (scallions), sliced into 5 cm (2 inch) lengths
4 garlic cloves, crushed
2 large red chillies, sliced in half lengthways
2 tablespoons fermented black beans, rinsed and crushed
1 kg (2 lb 4 oz) mussels, scrubbed and debearded

to serve
steamed rice

Place the sugar, soy sauce, Shaoxing rice wine and 60 ml (1/4 cup) water in a small bowl and stir to combine. Heat a large wok or wide flat saucepan until very hot, add the oil and when hot add the ginger, spring onion, garlic, chilli and black beans and stir for 30 seconds until aromatic. Add the mussels and toss to combine. Pour over the soy mixture, and cover. Cook covered for 2 to 5 minutes, shaking the pan, until the mussels open. Shake all the mussels, discarding any unopened ones, and sauce into a large warmed serving dish. Serve with steamed rice. Serves 4 as an entree or 2 as a main

saffron chicken skewers

2 large pinches saffron strands
250 g (1 cup) plain yoghurt
2 garlic cloves, crushed
2 tablespoons lemon juice
4 x 200 g (7 oz) chicken breasts, cut into
  three, lengthwise
1 teaspoon sumac, optional

sea salt
1 red onion, finely sliced, to garnish
flat-leaf (Italian) parsley leaves, to garnish

to serve
lemon cheeks
crispy salad (below)

Crush the saffron strands with the back of a spoon then steep in a bowl with 2 tablespoons of boiling water for 5 minutes. Place the saffron mixture, yoghurt, garlic and lemon juice in a bowl and whisk to combine. Add the chicken and turn until well coated in the marinade. Cover with plastic wrap and place in the refrigerator for 3 hours or overnight. Meanwhile, soak 12 wooden skewers in water for 30 minutes to stop them from burning during cooking.

Remove the chicken from the marinade and thread onto skewers. Cook on a barbecue or grill for 2 minutes each side. Sprinkle with the sumac, if using, salt and garnish with parsley and onion. Serve with lemon cheeks and crispy salad. Serves 4–6

crispy salad

2 heads of baby cos lettuce, washed
  and dried
8 small radishes, quartered
2 Lebanese (short) cucumbers, quartered
  and sliced
2 Roma (plum) tomatoes, chopped

dressing
60 ml (1/4 cup) extra virgin olive oil
2 tablespoons lemon juice
sea salt
freshly ground black pepper

Place the lettuce, radish and cucumber in a large bowl, cover with plastic wrap and chill for 30 minutes. This step is optional, but will make your salad lovely and crisp. Place the olive oil, lemon juice, salt and pepper in a small bowl and whisk to combine. Remove the salad from the refrigerator, add the tomatoes, pour over the dressing and toss to combine.

lobster with lime butter

60 ml (¹/4 cup) lime juice
125 g (4 oz) butter
2 large raw lobster tails
1 tablespoon olive oil
sea salt

freshly ground black pepper

to serve
green bean salad (below)

Place a baking tray in the oven and preheat to 220°C (425°F/Gas 7). To make the lime butter, heat the lime juice in a small saucepan over a medium heat. Add the butter and whisk constantly until melted. Set aside. Cut the lobster tails in half lengthways and season with salt and pepper. Place a large frying pan over a high heat, add the oil and arrange the lobsters cut-side down in the pan. Sear for 2 minutes, place the lobsters on the hot baking tray, drizzle with lime butter and roast for 10 to 15 minutes, or until the lobster flesh is opaque and just cooked. Arrange the lobster tails on a platter and serve with green bean salad. Serves 4

green bean salad

500 g (1 lb 2 oz) green beans, topped
1 teaspoon seeded mustard
60 ml (¹/4 cup) extra virgin olive oil
1 tablespoon red wine vinegar

sea salt
freshly ground black pepper
¹/2 red onion, finely sliced
20 g (1 cup) flat-leaf (Italian) parsley leaves

Blanch the beans in boiling water for 2 minutes, or until just tender and bright green in colour. Drain and refresh under cold water.

Place the mustard, olive oil and vinegar in a large bowl and whisk to combine. Season with salt and pepper. Add the beans, onion and parsley and gently toss to combine.

I like to serve everything separately on the table
and let the guests help themselves.

fish burritos

50 g (1 cup) roughly chopped coriander
   (cilantro) leaves and stems
2 teaspoons paprika
1 teaspoon cumin
1 small red chilli, seeded and chopped
1 teaspoon sea salt
freshly ground black pepper
zest of 1 lime
80 ml (1/3 cup) olive oil

750 g (1 lb 10 oz) snapper fillets, or other
   firm white fish, skin removed, and cut
   into strips

to serve
lime cheeks
8 fresh tortillas, warmed
cucumber salad (below)
lime mayonnaise (below)
baby cos lettuce leaves

Place all the ingredients except the fish in a blender or a food processor and process until a
paste forms. Place the fish in a bowl, add the paste and stir to combine. Leave to marinate for
15 minutes. Heat a non-stick frying pan over a high heat until hot, add some of the fish strips
in a single layer and cook for 2 minutes. Turn and cook on the other side for 1 minute, or until
the fish is opaque and just cooked. Remove from the pan and continue until all the fish has
been cooked. Place on a serving platter and garnish with lime cheeks.

While the fish is cooking, wrap the tortillas in foil and place in a 200°C (400°F/Gas 6) oven
for 5 minutes to warm through. To serve, place bowls of cucumber salad, lime mayonnaise
and lettuce on the table, along with the fish and tortillas. Serves 4

cucumber salad

1 telegraph (long) cucumber
250 g (1 punnet) cherry tomatoes, sliced
   in half
4 spring onions (scallions), sliced
handful of coriander (cilantro) leaves

1 teaspoon lime juice
1 small red chilli, seeded and sliced finely
1 teaspoon sea salt
1 teaspoon caster (superfine) sugar

Peel the cucumber and slice in half lengthways, remove the seeds with a teaspoon and slice
into 5 mm (1/4 inch) pieces. Place the remaining ingredients in a bowl and toss to combine.

lime mayonnaise

250 g (1 cup) whole egg mayonnaise
   (you can use skim milk yoghurt for a
   low-fat alternative)

finely grated zest of 1 lime
2 tablespoons lime juice
1 teaspoon sea salt

Place all the ingredients in a bowl and stir to combine. Refrigerate until needed.

caramel chicken

8 chicken thigh fillets, skinless, chopped in half
1 tablespoon vegetable oil
1 red onion, sliced
3 garlic cloves, sliced
freshly ground black pepper
60 ml (^{1}/4 cup) dark soy sauce
115 g (^{1}/2 cup) brown sugar
60 ml (^{1}/4 cup) fish sauce

to serve
steamed rice
steamed green vegetables, such as snow peas (mangetout),
    asparagus or Chinese broccoli

Place the chicken and oil in a bowl and toss to combine. Heat a large frying pan over a high heat until hot. Add the chicken, in two batches, and cook for 2 minutes on one side until lightly brown, turn and cook for another minute. Remove from the pan. Reduce the heat to medium and add a little extra oil if needed. Add the onion and garlic and cook for 5 minutes, stirring occasionally. Return the chicken to the pan, sprinkle liberally with black pepper, add the soy sauce and stir to combine. Cover the pan, reduce heat to low and cook for 10 minutes, stirring occasionally. Increase the heat to high, add the sugar and stir to combine. Cook uncovered for 3 to 4 minutes, or until the sauce is rich, dark and syrupy. Add the fish sauce and stir to combine. Place in a serving dish and serve with steamed rice and green vegetables. Serves 4

I don't bother to salt eggplants these days as I often don't notice much of a difference—anything to make life easier!

marinated lamb with spicy eggplant salad

1 teaspoon paprika
1/2 teaspoon cumin
2 garlic cloves, crushed
2 tablespoons olive oil
4 x 200 g (7 oz) lamb backstraps
sea salt
freshly ground black pepper

to serve
spicy eggplant salad (below)
coriander (cilantro) sprigs
plain yoghurt

Place the paprika, cumin, garlic and olive oil in a bowl and stir to combine. Trim the lamb of any excess fat and sinew then coat with the marinade. Cover with plastic wrap and place in the refrigerator to marinate for 2 hours, bringing to room temperature in the last 30 minutes.

Heat a frying pan over a high heat. Season the lamb with salt and pepper and cook for 3 to 4 minutes each side. Transfer the lamb to a plate, cover with foil and keep in a warm place for 10 minutes. Slice each lamb fillet on the diagonal into 2 cm (3/4 inch) pieces and serve with the spicy eggplant salad, coriander sprigs and yoghurt. Serves 4

spicy eggplant salad

2 large eggplant (aubergine)
2 tablespoons olive oil
3 garlic cloves, crushed
3 tablespoons chopped flat-leaf
   (Italian) parsley
3 tablespoons chopped coriander (cilantro)
2 tablespoons paprika
1 small red chilli, seeded and finely
   chopped

1/2 teaspoon ground cumin
2 tablespoons olive oil, extra
4 large Roma (plum) tomatoes, roughly
   chopped
1 teaspoon sea salt
1 tablespoon brown sugar
2 tablespoons lemon juice
1 tablespoon red wine vinegar
freshly ground black pepper

Cut into 1 cm (1/2 inch) thick slices. Preheat the oven to 200°C (400°F/Gas 6). Place the eggplant in a single layer in two baking trays and brush with olive oil on each side. Cook for 30 minutes, swapping the position of the trays halfway through. Remove from the oven. Sprinkle the eggplant with water if it is a little dry. Cool for 5 minutes, dice and place in a bowl. Add the garlic, parsley, coriander, paprika, chilli and cumin and stir to combine. Place the extra olive oil in a saucepan over a medium to high heat and add the tomatoes, salt and sugar. Cook for 10 minutes, add the eggplant mixture and cook for another 5 minutes. Remove from the heat and stir in the lemon juice, vinegar and black pepper. Serve warm.

I like to serve this dish with crispy roast potatoes.

grilled veal cutlets with lemon and caper dressing

4 x 225 g (8 oz) veal cutlets, 2 cm
   (3/4 inch) thick
2 tablespoons olive oil
sea salt
freshly ground black pepper

150 g (5 1/2 oz) wild rocket (arugula) leaves,
   or normal rocket (arugula) leaves
caper and lemon dressing (below)

to serve
crispy roast potatoes (page 15)

Place a large frying pan over a high heat. While the pan is heating, brush the cutlets with olive oil and sprinkle liberally with salt and pepper.

Place the cutlets in the pan, two at a time, and cook for 1 minute each side, or until lightly browned. Reduce the heat to medium and cook each side for another 3 minutes, or until cooked to your liking. Divide the rocket between four plates, top with a cutlet and drizzle over the lemon and caper dressing. Serve with crispy roast potatoes. Serves 4

lemon and caper dressing

60 ml (1/4 cup) lemon juice
60 ml (1/4 cup) extra virgin olive oil

2 tablespoons capers (packed in salt), rinsed
freshly ground black pepper

Place all the ingredients in a bowl and whisk until combined.

You only use the rind of preserved lemons. Make sure that you rinse them well—the flesh should just wash away.

barbecued fish with preserved lemon dressing and parsley salad

4 x 500 g (1 lb 2 oz) baby snappers
2 tablespoons olive oil
sea salt
freshly ground black pepper

to serve
preserved lemon dressing (below)
parsley salad (below)

Brush the fish with olive oil and season with salt and pepper. Make three diagonal slashes on both sides of each fish. Heat the barbecue or grill until very hot and cook for 4 minutes each side, or until the fish is opaque and just cooked.

Remove the fish to a serving dish and drizzle over the preserved lemon dressing. Serve with the parsley salad. Serves 4

preserved lemon dressing

60 ml (1/4 cup) extra virgin olive oil
freshly ground black pepper
1 tablespoon fresh oregano leaves

3 tablespoons finely sliced
    preserved lemon

Place the olive oil, 2 tablespoons .ater and pepper in a bowl and whisk to combine. Add the oregano and preserved lemon and stir to combine.

parsley salad

175 g (1 cup) fine grain burghul
60 g (1/2 cup) finely chopped spring onions
    (scallions)
20 g (1 cup) roughly chopped flat-leaf
    (Italian) parsley
80 ml (1/3 cup) olive oil
60 ml (1/4 cup) lemon juice

1 1/2 teaspoons ground cumin
1 green chilli, seeded and finely chopped
2 Lebanese (short) cucumbers, sliced in
    four lengthways and finely sliced
sea salt
freshly ground black pepper

Place the burghul in a fine sieve over the sink. Soak the burghul with lots of water, and let stand for 30 minutes. Squeeze out any remaining water before placing in a bowl with the remaining ingredients. Season to taste with salt and pepper then stir to combine.

Sea salt acts as an abrasive against the chilli and garlic and also helps to bring out the flavour.

stir-fried chicken with chilli and basil

4 garlic cloves
1 large red chilli
1/4 teaspoon sea salt
2 tablespoons vegetable oil
2 x 200 g (7 oz) skinless chicken breasts, sliced on the diagonal
300 g (10 1/2 oz) snake beans or green beans, cut into 3 cm (1 1/4 inch) lengths
   on the diagonal
2 tablespoons fish sauce
1 tablespoon dark soy sauce
1 tablespoon sugar
2 large red chillies, cut lengthways, seeds removed, extra
15 g (1/2 cup) Asian basil leaves, or regular basil

to serve
steamed jasmine rice

Roughly chop the garlic and chilli. Place in a mortar and pestle with the salt and pound into a paste. If you don't have a mortar and pestle, place the garlic and chilli on a chopping board, sprinkle with salt and finely mince with a knife, using the side to make a paste. Place a wok or a large non-stick frying pan over a high heat for 1 minute, heat the oil and add the garlic chilli paste. Stir-fry for 15 seconds until lightly golden. Add the chicken and beans. Cook, stirring, for about 5 minutes. Add the fish sauce, soy sauce, sugar and chilli and stir-fry for 30 seconds longer. Remove from the heat and stir through the basil. Serve immediately with steamed jasmine rice. Serves 2

If you can't find cherry tomatoes on the vine, use 2 punnets of cherry tomatoes instead.

lamb racks with breadcrumbs, parsley and lemon

3 thick slices wholemeal or sourdough bread
7 g (1/4 cup) finely chopped flat-leaf (Italian) parsley
finely grated zest of 1 lemon
1 garlic clove, crushed
60 ml (1/4 cup) olive oil
sea salt
freshly ground black pepper
2 x 8 French-trimmed lamb racks
olive oil, extra
2 tablespoons Dijon mustard
500 g (1 lb 2 oz) cherry tomatoes on the vine
4 garlic cloves, unpeeled (optional)

Preheat the oven to 180°C (350°F/Gas 4). Place the bread on a baking tray and toast for 20 minutes, or until lightly golden. Remove from the oven and leave to cool. Crumble the toasted bread with your hands or process in a food processor until breadcrumbs form. Place the breadcrumbs with the parsley, zest, garlic, olive oil, salt and pepper into a bowl and stir to combine.

Rub a little of the extra olive oil over the lamb racks. Season the lamb liberally with salt and pepper. Heat a large frying pan over a high heat for 2 minutes. Place the racks, fat-side down, in the pan and cook for 2 minutes. Remove to a baking tray.

Spread the top of the lamb racks with mustard and press on the breadcrumb mixture. Place the cherry tomatoes and the garlic in a separate baking tray with a little olive oil and put in the oven with the lamb. Cook for 25 to 30 minutes, or until the lamb is cooked and nicely pink. Remove the lamb from the oven and leave to rest in a baking tray loosely covered with foil for 5 minutes. Turn the oven off but leave the tomatoes in to keep warm. Cut each rack in half then serve with the roast tomatoes and garlic, if desired.

I like to serve this dish with pitta crisps—just break up pieces of pitta bread, drizzle with olive oil, sea salt, black pepper and paprika and bake for 10 to 12 minutes in a moderate oven until crisp.

chickpea stew with tomatoes and green chilli

2 tablespoons olive oil
1 red onion, finely sliced
3 garlic cloves, finely sliced
2 teaspoons freshly grated ginger
1 or 2 green chillies, to taste, seeded and finely chopped
1 teaspoon sea salt
2 x 400 g (14 oz) tins chickpeas, drained
1 teaspoon ground cumin
$1/2$ teaspoon turmeric, optional
freshly ground black pepper
500 g (2 punnets) cherry tomatoes, sliced in half
100 g ($3^1/2$ oz) baby English spinach leaves

to serve
plain yoghurt

Heat a large deep frying pan over a medium to high heat. Add the oil, onion, garlic, ginger, chilli and salt. Cook, stirring, for 5 minutes, or until the onions are soft. Add the chickpeas, 80 ml ($1/4$ cup) water, cumin, turmeric and pepper and cook for 5 minutes, or until the water evaporates. Add the tomatoes and cook for another 2 minutes to soften. Remove from the heat and taste for seasoning. Stir through the spinach and top with yoghurt. Serves 4 as a main or 8 as a side.

I find the best way to carve a chicken is first cut off the legs and thighs then chop them in half at the joint. Remove the breast and wings then slice in half. Arrange the chicken pieces on a platter and serve.

stuffed roast chicken

6 thick slices good-quality bread (I like
   wholemeal)
1 tablespoon olive oil
155 g (1 cup) roughly chopped onion
80 g (1/2 cup) chopped pancetta, bacon or
   prosciutto
finely grated zest of 1 lemon
1 tablespoon chopped sage or thyme leaves
7 g (1/4 cup) roughly chopped parsley

sea salt
freshly ground black pepper
1 egg, lightly beaten
1 x 1.5 kg (3 lb 5 oz) free-range chicken
1 tablespoon olive oil, extra

to serve
roast vegetables (below)
green salad (optional)

Preheat the oven to 220°C (425°F/Gas 7). Tear the bread roughly and place in a food processor and process until large breadcrumbs form. Place in a large bowl.

Place a frying pan over a medium heat. Put the olive oil in the pan, heat and add the onion. Cook for 3 minutes, stirring occasionally. Add the pancetta and cook for another 3 minutes. Remove the onion and pancetta and place in the bowl of breadcrumbs. Add the zest, sage, parsley, salt, pepper and egg and mix well to combine.

Wash the chicken and dry inside and out with paper towels. Fill the cavity with the stuffing mixture, then truss the chicken with kitchen string. Rub lightly with olive oil then season with salt and pepper.

Place the chicken in the oven, breast-side up, and cook for 15 minutes. Lower the heat to 180°C (350°F/Gas 4) and cook for another hour, or until the juices run clear when a skewer is inserted into the thickest part of the leg. Remove from the oven, loosely cover with foil and rest for 15 minutes before carving. Serve with a green salad, if desired, and the roasted vegetables. Serves 4

roast vegetables

1 kg (2 lb 4 oz) pumpkin, potato and sweet
   potato, cut into chunks
2 red onions, peeled and quartered

60 ml (1/4 cup) extra virgin olive oil
sea salt
freshly ground black pepper

Place all the ingredients in a bowl and toss to combine. Put in a baking dish, spreading the vegetables evenly, and bake at the same time as the chicken. Leave in the oven while the chicken is resting.

I love raw celery in salads. It's not used much these days, but I find it adds terrific texture and crunch.

roasted soy chicken with noodle salad

150 g (5¹/2 oz) fresh ginger, finely sliced
2 tablespoons caster (superfine) sugar
125 ml (¹/2 cup) oyster sauce
125 ml (¹/2 cup) Shaoxing rice wine, or
   dry sherry
1 teaspoon sesame oil

4 x 250 g (9 oz) chicken breasts
2 spring onions (scallions), cut diagonally,
   to garnish

to serve
noodle salad (below)

Place the ginger, sugar, oyster sauce, Shaoxing rice wine and sesame oil in a large bowl and stir to combine. Add the chicken, cover with plastic wrap and marinate for at least 3 hours in the refrigerator, bringing to room temperature in the last 30 minutes.

Preheat the oven to 220°C (425°F/Gas 7). Sear the chicken, skin-side down, with a little oil in a frying pan on medium to high heat. Remove the chicken when golden and place skin-side up on a baking tray. Brush lightly with the marinade and cook for 10 to 12 minutes. Slice each chicken breast into two. Place on a serving plate, pour over pan juices, garnish with spring onions and serve immediately with the noodle salad. Serves 4

noodle salad

1 tablespoon sesame oil
80 ml (¹/3 cup) dark soy sauce
2 tablespoons rice vinegar
2 teaspoons brown sugar
200 g (7 oz) egg noodles, boiled according
   to manufacturer's instructions, drained
   and refreshed under cold water

6 spring onions (scallions), finely sliced
200 g (7 oz) snow peas (mangetout),
   blanched and refreshed with cold water
2 sticks celery, finely julienned
1 tablespoon toasted sesame seeds

Place the sesame oil, soy sauce, vinegar and sugar in a large bowl and stir to combine. Add the noodles, spring onion, snow peas and celery then sprinkle sesame seeds over the top.

grilled white fish with corn salsa

60 ml (1/4 cup) olive oil
1 teaspoon paprika
1 teaspoon ground cumin
4 x 200 g (7 oz) firm white fish fillets such
    as blue eye or snapper, skin removed
sea salt

freshly ground black pepper

to serve
coriander (cilantro) sprigs, to garnish
corn salsa (below)
lime cheeks

Place the olive oil, paprika and cumin in a bowl and whisk to combine. Place the fish on a plate and pour over the marinade, turning the fish so it is evenly coated. Season with salt and pepper.

Heat a barbecue or grill and place a large frying pan over a medium to high heat until hot. Place the fish in the pan and cook for 2 to 3 minutes. Turn and cook on the other side for 2 to 3 minutes, or until the fish is opaque and just cooked.

Garnish with coriander sprigs and serve on individual serving plates with the corn salsa and lime cheeks. Serves 4

corn salsa

3 tablespoons olive oil
400 g (2 cups) fresh corn kernels
200 g (7 oz) green beans, sliced thinly
sea salt
freshly ground black pepper

4 spring onions (scallions), finely chopped
10 g (1/2 cup) mint leaves, whole
1 green chilli, chopped
2 tablespoons lime juice

Place a frying pan over a medium to high heat and add the oil. Once the oil is hot, add the corn and beans. Season with salt and pepper and cook for 3 minutes. Place the spring onions, mint, chilli and lime juice in a bowl and add the corn mixture. Stir to combine.

spicy beef with coriander relish

80 ml (¹/3 cup) Shaoxing rice wine, or
   dry sherry
60 ml (¹/4 cup) oyster sauce
60 ml (¹/4 cup) light soy sauce
2 tablespoons caster (superfine) sugar
1 tablespoon sesame oil

4 x 200 g (7 oz) sirloin steaks

to serve
200 g (7 oz) snow peas (mangetout)
steamed rice
coriander relish (below)

Place the Shaoxing rice wine, oyster sauce, soy sauce, sugar and sesame oil in a large bowl and stir until the sugar is dissolved. Add the steaks then cover with plastic wrap and place in the refrigerator to marinate for 2 hours, bringing to room temperature in the last 30 minutes.

Meanwhile, prepare the coriander relish while the steaks are marinating.

Preheat a frying pan or barbecue until hot. Sear the steaks for 2 minutes each side, by which time they will be done if you like rare steak. Continue cooking over a medium heat for 1 to 2 minutes on each side for medium and 2 to 3 minutes on each side for well done.

Remove the steaks from the pan and allow to rest for 5 minutes in a warm place. Lightly blanch the snow peas in boiling water then plunge into cold water and drain well. Slice each steak into 1 cm (¹/2 inch) slices, top with a little relish and serve with steamed rice and snow peas. Serve with the coriander relish. Serves 4

coriander relish

50 g (1 cup) chopped coriander (cilantro),
   including stems
60 ml (¹/4 cup) vegetable oil
2 tablespoons lime juice
1 large red chilli, seeded and finely minced

1 tablespoon fish sauce
1 teaspoon caster (superfine) sugar
freshly ground black pepper

Place all the ingredients in a small bowl and stir to combine.

Remove the backbone from the chicken by cutting either side of the bone. Flatten out chicken with the palm of your hand, and remove the breastbone by cutting on either side of the bone. Skewer to secure the joints.

marinated coriander chicken

2 small free-range chickens, around 1.2 kg
(approximately 2 lb 11 oz) each, cut
into two
100 g (2 cups) coriander (cilantro) stems
and leaves, roughly chopped
2 teaspoons black peppercorns
2 teaspoons sea salt
3 garlic cloves
2 tablespoons lime juice
60 ml ($^1/_4$ cup) vegetable oil

to serve
coriander (cilantro) sprigs
cucumber relish (below)
lime cheeks

Soak eight wooden skewers in cold water for 30 minutes to stop them from burning during cooking. Slash each chicken half a few times to allow the marinade flavours to penetrate. Run a wooden skewer through the flesh of each chicken piece to secure to the joints, and place in a large baking dish.

Place the coriander, peppercorns, salt, garlic, lime juice and oil in a blender or food processor and process until smooth. Pour the marinade over the chicken pieces, rubbing well into the flesh, and cover with plastic wrap. Place in the refrigerator to marinate for 2 hours, bringing to room temperature in the last 30 minutes.

Preheat the barbecue to high. Place the chicken halves on the barbecue and cook, cut-side down, for 6 to 8 minutes. Turn and cook flesh-side down for a further 5 to 6 minutes, or until the chicken is cooked through. Alternatively, preheat the oven to 220°C (425°F/Gas 7). Place the chicken on a baking tray, skin-side up, and bake for 30 to 35 minutes. Garnish with coriander sprigs and serve with the cucumber relish and lime cheeks.

cucumber relish

125 ml ($^1/_2$ cup) rice vinegar, or white vinegar
115 g ($^1/_2$ cup) caster (superfine) sugar
1 Lebanese (short) cucumber, quartered
lengthways and finely sliced
2 red Asian shallots or $^1/_2$ red onion,
peeled and finely sliced
1 large red chilli, seeded and finely sliced

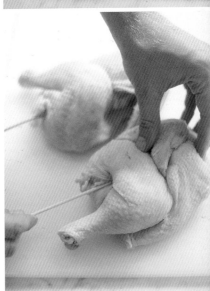

Place the vinegar and sugar in a small saucepan over a medium heat, and stir until the sugar has dissolved. Remove from the heat and cool. Pour into a bowl, add the cucumber, shallot and chilli and stir to combine.

Make this simple ginger tomato sauce by frying a little chilli, ginger and garlic in olive oil until fragrant. Add 600 g (1 lb 5 oz) chopped tomatoes and cook for 25 minutes.

marinated lamb cutlets

1 teaspoon crushed coriander seeds
1 teaspoon crushed fennel seeds
1/2 teaspoon ground cumin
1/4 teaspoon dried chilli flakes
3 garlic cloves, sliced
3 tablespoons extra virgin olive oil
sea salt

freshly ground black pepper
12 French-trimmed lamb cutlets

to serve
ginger tomato sauce (above)
warm lentil and rice pilaff (below)
lemon wedges

Place all the ingredients except the lamb cutlets in a bowl and stir until combined. Add the lamb to the marinade and toss to combine. Cover with plastic wrap and place in the refrigerator to marinate for 2 hours, bringing to room temperature in the last 30 minutes.

Heat a frying pan over a high heat for 1 minute. Add the cutlets and cook for 1 to 2 minutes, turn and cook for another minute for medium rare. Serve with the ginger tomato sauce, warm lentil and rice pilaff and lemon wedges. Serves 4

warm lentil and rice pilaff

185 g (1 cup) lentils du Puy
200 g (1 cup) long-grain rice
1/2 lemon
2 tablespoons extra virgin olive oil
1 large onion, finely sliced

sea salt
freshly ground black pepper
15 g (1/2 cup) roughly chopped flat-leaf
   (Italian) parsley

Bring a large pot of water to the boil, add the lentils and cook for 10 minutes. Add the rice and lemon and cook for another 12 to 15 minutes, or until the lentils and rice are tender. Drain, discarding the lemon, and place in a serving bowl.

Meanwhile, heat a frying pan over a medium to high heat. When hot, add the oil and onion, and cook for 10 to 12 minutes, or until the onion is a rich golden brown (don't worry if they catch a bit), stirring frequently. Remove from the heat.

Sprinkle the pilaff with salt, lots of pepper, parsley and half of the cooked onion. Stir to combine. Top with the remaining onion and serve.

beef and mushroom pot pies

2 tablespoons plain (all-purpose) flour

2 teaspoons paprika

1 teaspoon sea salt

freshly ground black pepper

1.5 kg (3 lb 5 oz) chuck or blade steak, cut into 2 cm (3/4 inch) chunks

1 x 425 g (15 oz) can chopped tomatoes

5 garlic cloves, sliced

2 red onions, cut in half and finely sliced

1 stick celery, finely chopped

250 ml (1 cup) red wine

1 teaspoon thyme leaves, chopped

300 g (101/2 oz) button mushrooms

30 g (1/2 cup) flat-leaf (Italian) parsley, roughly chopped

1 x 375 g (13 oz) packet puff pastry

1 egg yolk, lightly beaten

to serve

simple spiced tomato relish (below)

Preheat the oven to 180°C (350°F/Gas 4). Place the flour and paprika in a bowl and stir to combine. Season with salt and pepper. Add the beef and toss until it is covered in flour. Place in an ovenproof casserole dish. Add the tomato, garlic, onion, celery, red wine and thyme and stir. Cover and cook for 11/2 hours, stirring occasionally. Add the mushrooms, cover and return to to the oven. Cook, stirring occasionally, for 1 hour, or until the sauce is thickened slightly and the beef and mushrooms are tender. Remove from the oven and stir through the parsley. The filling can be made up to a day in advance to this stage. Increase the oven temperature to 200°C (400°F/Gas 6). On a lightly floured surface, roll out the pastry until 3 mm (1/4 inch) thick. Using the top of a 325 ml (11/2 cup) ovenproof ramekin as a template, cut out six circles of pastry, leaving 1 cm (1/2 inch) extra around the circumference.

Divide the pie filling into six 325 ml (11/2 cup) ovenproof ramekins and cover with pastry, pushing down the edges around the rim. Make a cut in the pastry top with a sharp knife to allow any steam to escape and brush with the egg yolk. Pies can be made and refrigerated in advance to this stage. Bake for 20 to 25 minutes or until the pastry is lightly golden. Serve with the simple spiced tomato relish or store-bought relish. Serves 6

simple spiced tomato relish

2 tablespoons olive oil

1 teaspoon mustard seeds

6 curry leaves, optional

1 red chilli, seeded and finely chopped

1 garlic clove, finely sliced

600 g (1 lb 5 oz) tomatoes, roughly chopped

1 tablespoon balsamic vinegar

1 tablespoon brown sugar

30 g (1/4 cup) sultanas, soaked in boiling water for 10 minutes, and drained

sea salt

freshly ground black pepper

Heat a small saucepan over a medium to high heat. Add the olive oil, mustard seeds, curry leaves, chilli and garlic and cook, stirring, until fragrant, about 30 seconds. Add the tomato, vinegar, brown sugar, sultanas, salt and pepper. Bring to the boil then reduce to a simmer. Cook, stirring occasionally, for·20 to 25 minutes, or until the tomato is pulpy. Remove from the heat and allow to cool before serving.

glazed duck with pear and rocket salad

2.5–3 kg (5 lb 8 oz–6 lb 12 oz) duck
1 orange, sliced in half
1 red onion, quartered
2.5 cm (1 inch) piece of fresh ginger,
    roughly sliced
sea salt
freshly ground black pepper
90 g (¹/4 cup) honey
2 teaspoons ground cumin

2 teaspoons ground cinnamon
1 tablespoon orange juice

to serve
mini potato gratins (below)
150 g (1 bunch) rocket (arugula)
2 pears, finely sliced

Preheat the oven to 120°C (250°F/Gas 1). Remove the parson's nose and a small amount of the surrounding area as this is where the oil glands are located and they can cause an unpleasant flavour to permeate the duck. The neck and the last two joints of the wings should also be removed. Rinse the duck inside and out then dry well with paper towels. Season liberally with salt and pepper both inside and out and place the orange, onion and ginger in the cavity and truss legs with kitchen string. Carefully prick the duck skin all over, but avoid piercing the flesh by inserting a very fine skewer into the skin at an angle almost parallel to the duck so you are only piercing skin and fat.

Put the honey, cumin, cinnamon and orange juice in a small bowl, stir to combine then set aside. Place the duck, breast-side up, on a rack in a baking dish and place in the oven. Roast the duck for 2 hours. Remove from the oven, increase the heat to 200°C (400°F/Gas 6) then return the duck to the oven. Cook for 40 minutes, brushing the orange glaze over the duck 15 minutes before the end of cooking time.

Remove from the oven and serve with mini potato gratins and a simple salad of rocket leaves and finely sliced pear. Serves 6

mini potato gratins

600 g (1 lb 5 oz) potatoes, peeled and very
    finely sliced
185 ml (³/4 cup) cream

sea salt
freshly ground black pepper

Preheat the oven to 200°C (400°F/Gas 6). Cut a piece of baking paper into 16 strips 15 x 2 cm (6 x ³/4 inch). Line six 125 ml (¹/2 cup) muffin tins with the strips, in a cross pattern with strips overlapping on each side. This will create little handles to remove your gratins with.

Place all the ingredients in a bowl and toss to combine. Layer the potatoes in the muffin tins and pour over any remaining liquid. Place in the oven and cook for 40 minutes.

This salad is also a fabulous accompaniment to the marinated coriander chicken (page 147) or other Thai inspired dishes.

coconut fish with cucumber salad

250 ml (1 cup) fish or chicken stock

1 x 400 ml (1¹/₃ cups) tin coconut milk

1 tablespoon fish sauce

1 tablespoon caster (superfine) sugar

2–3 makrut (kaffir) lime leaves

1 stalk lemon grass, bruised

1 small red chilli, split lengthways

4 x 175 g (6 oz) firm white fish fillets such as snapper or barramundi, skin removed

1 tablespoon lime juice

extra makrut (kaffir) lime leaves, finely sliced, to garnish

to serve

steamed rice

cucumber salad (below)

Place the stock, coconut milk, fish sauce, sugar, lime leaves, lemon grass and chilli in a large pot over a medium to high heat. Boil for 10 minutes, then lower the heat and bring to a simmer. Add the fish and poach for 2 to 3 minutes, or until the fish starts to flake when lightly pressed with the edge of a fork. Remove the fish from the pan, cover and set aside. Reduce the sauce for another 5 minutes over high heat until thickened slightly. Strain and stir in 1 tablespoon lime juice. Pour over the fish. Any leftover poaching liquid can be served in small soup bowls as a delicious accompaniment. Garnish with extra lime leaves and serve with steamed rice and the cucumber salad.

cucumber salad

2 large chillies, seeded and finely sliced on the diagonal

30 g (¹/₂ cup) picked coriander (cilantro) leaves

3 red Asian shallots or ¹/₂ small red onion, finely sliced

5 g (¹/₄ cup) mint leaves

20 snow peas (mangetout), blanched and finely sliced

2 Lebanese (small) cucumbers, cut in half lengthways and sliced on the diagonal

dressing (below)

Place all the ingredients except dressing in a bowl and cover with plastic wrap. Refrigerate until serving. Toss through dressing just before serving.

dressing

2 tablespoons lime juice

2 tablespoons fish sauce

1 teaspoon caster (superfine) sugar

1 small red chilli, finely chopped (optional)

Place all the ingredients in a small bowl and stir to combine.

To make a simple raita just wilt some English spinach in a frying pan. Leave to cool then mix with plain yoghurt, lemon juice, sea salt and black pepper.

lamb with saffron rice

250 g (1 cup) plain yoghurt
2 garlic cloves, crushed
1 tablespoon fresh ginger, grated
1 teaspoon ground turmeric
1 teaspoon ground cumin
1 teaspoon ground coriander
2 tablespoons lemon juice
4 x 200 g (7 oz) lamb backstraps

sea salt
freshly ground black pepper

to serve
mint leaves, to garnish
saffron rice (below)
spinach raita (above)

Place all the ingredients, except the lamb, salt and pepper in a bowl and stir well to combine. Add the lamb then cover with plastic wrap and place in the refrigerator to marinate for 2 hours, bringing to room temperature in the last 30 minutes.

Preheat the oven to 240°C (475°F/Gas 9). Place the lamb on a baking tray, season with salt and pepper, and cook in the oven for 8 to 10 minutes, or until cooked to your liking. Remove from the oven, cover with foil and rest for 5 minutes. Cut the lamb into slices on the diagonal and place on a serving plate. Garnish with mint leaves and serve with saffron rice and spinach raita.

saffron rice

1 tablespoon vegetable oil
1 teaspoon butter
1 onion, finely sliced
1 teaspoon sea salt

500 g (2 1/2 cups) basmati rice
2 pinches saffron threads
30 g (1/4 cup) sultanas
2 tablespoons toasted flaked almonds

Place a large pan with a tight-fitting lid over a medium to high heat. Add the oil, butter, onion and salt and cook for 5 to 10 minutes, or until lightly coloured. Add the rice and stir for 1 minute. Add 1 litre (4 cups) boiling water, saffron and sultanas, and bring to the boil. Cover, reduce heat to low, and cook for 10 minutes. Turn off the heat and leave the pan for 10 minutes. Do not lift the lid as it will interrupt the cooking process. Serve immediately with toasted flaked almonds over the top.

Sometimes if I don't have enough time to make my own mayonnaise I cheat a little and make this delicious version. Simply use 1 cup (250 g) of good-quality mayonnaise and mix through shredded basil leaves, sea salt, black pepper and a little extra lemon juice. It takes only minutes.

slow-cooked salmon salad with fresh basil mayonnaise

250 g (1 punnet) cherry tomatoes
3 garlic cloves, unpeeled and bruised with
   the side of a knife
60 ml (1/4 cup) extra virgin olive oil
4 x 180 g (6 oz) salmon fillets, skin removed
2 tablespoons extra virgin olive oil, extra
sea salt

300 g (10 oz) green beans, topped but not
   tailed, blanched
30 g (1 cup) watercress leaves
175 g (1/2 cup) black olives
25 g (1/2 cup) basil leaves

to serve
fresh basil mayonnaise (below)

Preheat the oven to 160°C (315°F/Gas 2–3). Put the tomatoes and garlic in a small ovenproof dish and pour over the olive oil. Place in the oven and bake for 35 minutes. Remove from the oven, set aside, and reduce the oven temperature to 120°C (250°F/ Gas 1–2). Place the fish in an ovenproof dish and pour over the extra oil. Rub the oil over the fish so it is coated evenly. Sprinkle with salt and place in the oven and cook for 35 minutes. Remove from the oven and leave to rest for 10 minutes.

While the salmon is resting, divide the beans evenly between four serving plates and top with watercress, tomatoes, olives and basil. Break the salmon into pieces and place on top. Serve with the basil mayonnaise in a separate bowl. Serves 4

fresh basil mayonnaise

2 egg yolks
2 tablespoons lemon juice
sea salt

freshly ground black pepper
250 ml (1 cup) canola oil
15 g (1/4 cup) shredded basil leaves

Place the egg yolks, lemon juice, salt and pepper in a bowl and whisk until combined. Add the oil drop by drop, whisking constantly. When the mayonnaise starts to thicken, add the oil in a steady stream until it is fully incorporated. Stir the basil leaves through.

roasted spatchcock with spicy potatoes

4 x 500–750 g (1–1½ lb) spatchcocks,
   halved
2 tablespoons extra virgin olive oil
sea salt
freshly ground black pepper

to serve
spicy potatoes (below)
orange and watercress salad (below)

Preheat the oven to 220°C (425°F/Gas 7). Cut the spatchcock through the breastbone with a sharp knife or poultry shears and flatten out with palm of your hand. Cut down either side of the spatchcock's backbone and remove. Place the spatchcock in a baking dish and rub the skin with olive oil. Sprinkle with salt and pepper. Cook for 25 to 30 minutes, or until golden. Rest for 5 minutes before serving. Serve with spicy potatoes and orange and watercress salad. Serves 4

spicy potatoes

1 kg (2 lb) potatoes
2 tablespoons olive oil
1 tablespoon tomato paste
2 tablespoons olive oil, extra

1 tablespoon red wine vinegar
2 teaspoons paprika
½ teaspoon Tabasco sauce, or to taste
sea salt

Preheat the oven to 220°C (425°F/Gas 7). Peel and roughly dice the potatoes, about 1.5 cm (5/8 inch) in size. Place in a bowl and toss with olive oil. Place on a baking tray and cook, turning halfway through, for 50 minutes, or until golden and crispy. Remove from the oven. Combine the tomato paste, extra olive oil, vinegar, paprika, Tabasco and salt in a bowl and stir to combine. Add the roasted potatoes and toss to combine just before serving.

orange and watercress salad

4 oranges
1 red onion, finely sliced
30 g (1 cup) watercress stems

extra virgin olive oil, for drizzling
sea salt
freshly ground black pepper

Cut the top and bottom off each orange. Stand the orange on one end on a cutting board and, following the curve of the orange, cut away the skin and pith with a sharp knife. Cut each orange, widthways, into 5 mm (1/4 inch) slices. Arrange the orange, onion and watercress on a plate. Drizzle with the olive oil and sprinkle with salt and pepper.

dessert

dessert

'Sweet things have a bad reputation but I'm a great fan of moderation and there's nothing wrong with the occasional bit of butter and sugar. Like breakfast, desserts are one of the real pleasures that have been sacrificed in an effort to cram more into a day.

But most of us love the indulgence of dessert and taking the time to prepare something, however simple, is valuable in itself. To me, dessert is something to linger over. It provides the ideal moment for savouring the day and incites some of the best conversations, certainly the best compliments!

As a cook, nothing gives me more satisfaction than making sweet things for people to enjoy.'

Sometimes I find it hard to remove the stone from plums. My solution? I cut as closely to the stone as possible to create 'cheeks' instead of halves.

yoghurt pannacotta with rose-scented plums

375 ml (1 1/2 cups) cream
115 g (1/2 cup) caster (superfine) sugar
1 vanilla bean, split lengthways
10 g (1/4 oz) sachet of gelatine powder
500 g (2 cups) skim milk yoghurt

to serve
rose-scented plums (below)

Place the cream and sugar in a saucepan over a medium heat. Using the point of a knife, scrape the vanilla bean seeds into the saucepan before adding the entire bean. Stir until the sugar is dissolved, then just bring to the boil before removing from the heat. Discard the vanilla bean. Pour 125 ml (1/2 cup) of the cream mixture into a small bowl, sprinkle the gelatine powder over the top and whisk with a fork until smooth. Pour back into the saucepan and stir until the gelatine has completely dissolved. (If you wish to use gelatine leaves instead, follow the manufacturer's instructions.) Add the yoghurt and whisk until smooth. Strain the mixture through a fine sieve and divide between eight 125 ml (1/2 cup) moulds, cover with plastic wrap and chill for 3 hours, or until just set.

To serve, dip each mould into hot water for a few seconds, making sure the water only comes halfway up the sides. Place a plate on top and invert the pannacotta. Serve immediately with the rose-scented plums and a spoonful of plum syrup. Serves 8

rose-scented plums

115 g (1/2 cup) caster (superfine) sugar
1 tablespoon rose-water

8 ripe plums, sliced

Place the sugar and rose-water into a large deep frying pan with 500 ml (2 cups) water. Stir gently over a low heat until the sugar dissolves. Increase the heat to high and bring the syrup to the boil. Boil rapidly for 1 minute then add the plums. Allow the syrup to come back to the boil then reduce to a simmer. Cook, stirring occasionally, for 8 to 10 minutes, or until the fruit is tender. Remove the plums, increase the heat and boil the syrup for a few minutes or until reduced. Pour over the plums and allow to cool before serving.

baked brown sugar custards

5 egg yolks
80 g (1/3 cup) brown sugar
500 ml (2 cups) milk
3 teaspoons natural vanilla extract

Preheat the oven to 160°C (315°F/Gas 2–3). Place the egg yolks and sugar in a bowl and whisk to combine. Place the milk and vanilla in a saucepan over medium heat and bring to the boil. Remove from the heat and gradually add the milk to the eggs, whisking constantly. Skim off any foam that rises to the top.

Place four 250 ml (1 cup) ovenproof ramekins into a baking dish. Divide the mixture between the ramekins. Pour hot water into the baking dish halfway up the sides of the ramekins and cover with foil. Bake for 45 to 50 minutes, or until the custards are just set. Remove the custards from the baking dish and leave to cool slightly before chilling for 2 hours. Serves 4

This trifle is heavily inspired by one served at a fabulous restaurant that Sydney used to have called Osteria Moana. They used pandoro which is a traditional Italian cake made for Christmas.

blueberry trifle

55 g (^{1}/4 cup) caster (superfine) sugar
1 tablespoon lemon juice
250 g (9 oz) blueberries
5 eggs, separated
115 g (^{1}/2 cup) caster (superfine) sugar, extra
1 vanilla bean, split lengthways, or 1 teaspoon natural vanilla extract
250 g (9 oz) mascarpone cheese
^{1}/2 pandoro, or 1 sponge cake, cut into 4 cm (1^1/2 inch) slices
185 ml (^{3}/4 cup) Marsala
45 g (^{1}/3 cup) flaked almonds, toasted

Place the sugar, lemon juice and 60 ml (^{1}/4 cup) water in a small saucepan over a medium heat. Stir until the sugar is dissolved then bring to the boil. Add the blueberries, reduce the heat to low and simmer for 5 minutes. Leave to cool.

While the syrup is cooling, place the egg yolks and extra sugar in a bowl and beat until the mixture is pale and creamy. Using the point of a knife, scrape the vanilla bean seeds into the bowl. Add the mascarpone and beat until smooth.

Place the egg whites in a clean, dry stainless steel bowl and whisk until soft peaks form. Using a large metal spoon, fold lightly through the mascarpone mixture in two batches.

Line a 2 litre (8 cup) serving bowl with a layer of pandoro or sponge cake, moisten with roughly a quarter of the Marsala, top with a quarter of the blueberries and syrup, and a quarter of the mascarpone mixture. Repeat the layering, reserving 2 tablespoons of the blueberries and syrup for garnishing, until you finish with a layer of the mascarpone mixture. Cover and refrigerate for 6 hours, or overnight, to allow the flavour to develop.

Remove the trifle from the refrigerator, drizzle over the reserved blueberries and syrup, and sprinkle with toasted flaked almonds. Serves 6 to 8

The trick to making a smooth clear caramel is to stir only until the sugar dissolves into the water, then leave to cook undisturbed. If you keep stirring, the caramel will crystalize and become grainy.

semifreddo with caramel figs

6 egg yolks
80 g (1/3 cup) caster (superfine) sugar
185 ml (3/4 cup) Marsala
finely grated zest of 1 lemon
1/2 teaspoon natural vanilla extract
375 ml (11/2 cups) cream, lightly whipped

to serve
caramel figs (below)

Place the egg yolks, sugar, Marsala, zest and vanilla in a heatproof bowl over a saucepan of simmering water, making sure the bowl does not touch the water. Whisk for 5 to 6 minutes, or until the mixture is fluffy and almost doubled in volume. Remove from the heat and allow to cool, whisking occasionally. Fold in the cream, then pour into a 20 x 11 cm (8 x 41/2 inch) loaf tin. Freeze for 4 hours.

Remove the semifreddo from freezer, leave for 5 minutes then turn out onto a platter. Cut into slices and serve with the caramel figs. Serves 6 to 8

caramel figs

230 g (1 cup) caster (superfine) sugar
4 figs, halved

Put the sugar and 80 ml (1/3 cup) water in a small saucepan and place over a medium to high heat, swirling (not stirring!) the pan gently until the caramel is golden. Remove from the heat. Using a fork, dip the fig halves in the caramel, making sure they are coated evenly. Be very careful as the caramel is extremely hot. Remove figs to a tray lined with baking paper. Leave the caramel to harden for 10 minutes and serve. Do not refrigerate as the toffee will soften.

chocolate sauce 1

125 g (4^1/$_2$ oz) good-quality chocolate
185 ml (^{3}/$_4$ cup) cream

Place the chocolate and cream in a heatproof bowl over a saucepan of simmering water, making sure the bowl does not touch the water. Stir for 2 minutes, or until the chocolate has almost melted. Remove from the heat and keep stirring until all lumps have melted and the mixture is smooth. Cool slightly before serving. Makes 315 ml (1^1/$_4$ cups)

chocolate sauce 2

115 g (^{1}/$_2$ cup) caster (superfine) sugar
60 g (^{1}/$_2$ cup) good-quality cocoa
125 ml (^{1}/$_2$ cup) cream

Place the sugar and 250 ml (1 cup) water in a small saucepan and place over a high heat. Stir until dissolved and bring to the boil. Add the cocoa and cream and whisk to combine. Reduce the heat and bring to a simmer. Cook for 5 minutes, stirring occasionally. Cool for 15 minutes before serving. Makes 440 ml (1^3/$_4$ cups)

easy caramel sauce

95 g (^{1}/$_2$ cup) brown sugar
250 ml (1 cup) cream
1 teaspoon natural vanilla extract
15 g (^{1}/$_2$ oz) butter

Place all the ingredients in a small saucepan over a medium heat, stir to combine and bring to a slow boil. Stir occasionally for 5 minutes, or until thick and syrupy. Makes 375 ml (1^1/$_2$ cups)

strawberry sauce

250 g (1 punnet) ripe strawberries, hulled
1 tablespoon lemon juice
1^1/$_2$ tablespoons caster (superfine) sugar

Place all the ingredients in a food processor and process until a sauce forms. For a finer texture, you can pass the sauce through a fine sieve. Makes 315 ml (1^1/$_4$ cups)

Raspberries also work very well in this sauce recipe. You could use frozen berries—just thaw slightly before blending.

little lemon puddings with yoghurt and blackberries

50 g (1³/4 oz) unsalted butter
finely grated zest of 1 lemon
115 g (¹/2 cup) caster (superfine) sugar
2 eggs, separated
40 g (¹/3 cup) plain (all-purpose) flour, sifted
300 ml (1¹/4 cups) milk
2 tablespoons lemon juice

to serve
plain yoghurt
250 g (1 punnet) blackberries
icing (confectioners') sugar, for dusting

Preheat the oven to 180°C (350°F/Gas 4). Place the butter, zest and sugar in a bowl and beat until pale and creamy. Add the egg yolks, one at a time, beating well after each addition. Fold through the flour then gradually add the milk in a steady stream, whisking lightly to combine. Add the lemon juice and mix to combine. The mixture will look slightly curdled.

Place the egg whites in a clean, dry stainless steel bowl and whisk until stiff peaks form. Using a large metal spoon, fold lightly through the pudding batter. Pour the batter into four 250 ml (1 cup) ovenproof ramekins and place on a baking tray. Bake for 15 minutes, or until lightly browned. Place a dollop of yoghurt and the blackberries on top then dust with icing sugar. Serves 4

GIRASOLE

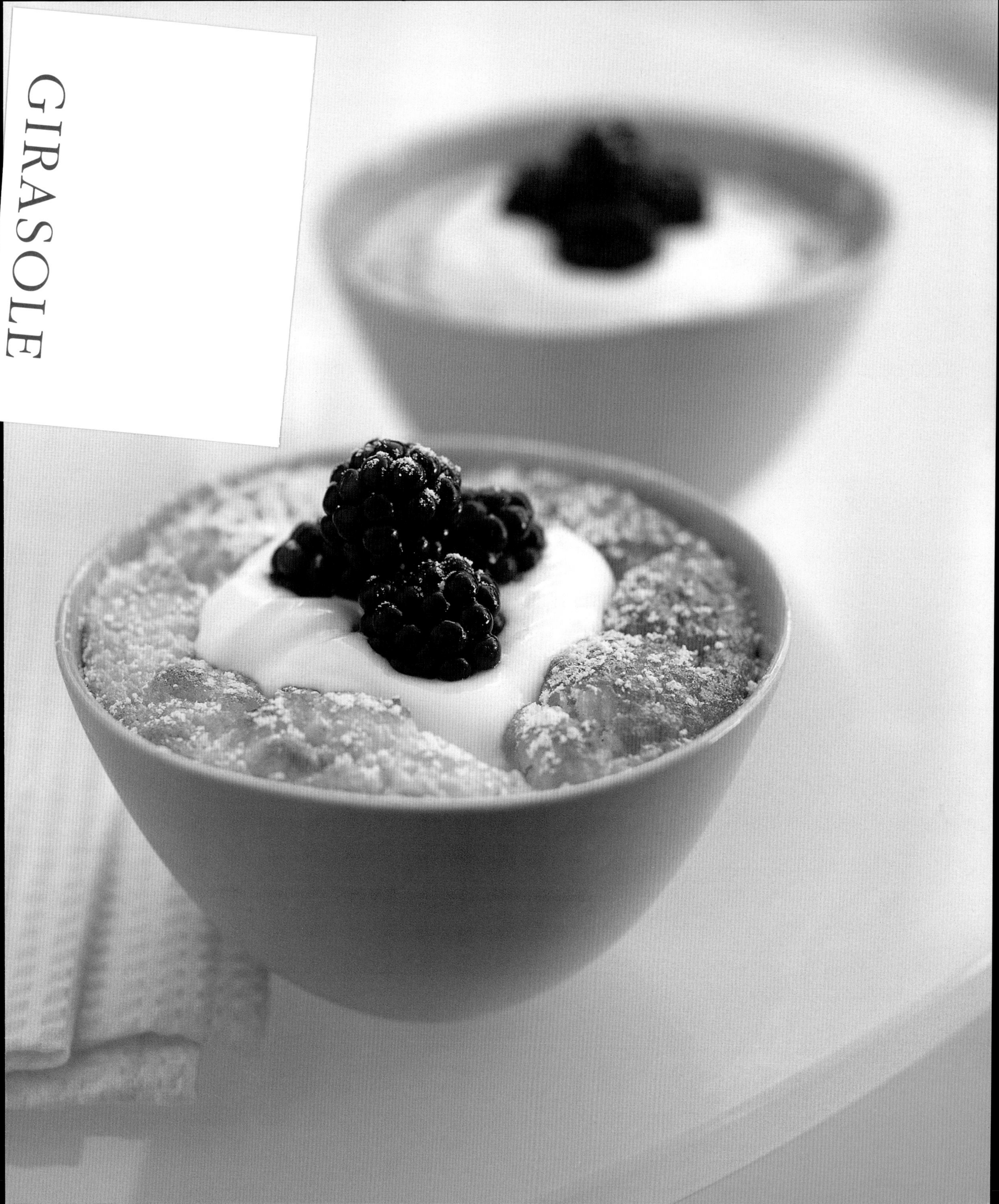

passionfruit crepes

90 g (3/4 cup) plain (all-purpose) flour
1 egg, lightly beaten
250 ml (1 cup) milk
20 g (3/4 oz) unsalted butter, melted
a pinch of salt
extra butter, for greasing the pan

to serve
icing (confectioners') sugar, for dusting
passionfruit curd (below)
vanilla ice cream

Place the flour into a large bowl, then add the egg, milk, melted butter and salt. Whisk until the batter is smooth. Chill for 1 hour before cooking.

Meanwhile, prepare the passionfruit curd while the crepe batter is resting.

Preheat the oven to 120°C (250°F/Gas 1). Heat a non-stick frying pan over a medium heat. Brush a little butter over the pan. Ladle 2 tablespoons of batter into the pan and tilt and swirl the pan to quickly and evenly spread the batter. After a minute, lift the outer edge of the crepe and flip, then cook for a couple of seconds on the other side. Transfer to a plate and keep warm in the oven while cooking the rest of the crepes.

Fold the crepes into quarters and dust with icing sugar. Serve with a dollop of passionfruit curd and vanilla ice cream. Makes 12

passionfruit curd

2 eggs
125 ml (1/2 cup) passionfruit pulp

80 g (1/3 cup) caster (superfine) sugar
60 g (2 1/2 oz) unsalted butter, softened

Place the eggs, passionfruit and sugar in a heatproof bowl over a saucepan of simmering water, making sure the bowl does not touch the water. Stir continually with a wooden spoon for 7 to 8 minutes, or until the mixture is thick, then remove from the heat and gradually whisk in the butter. Leave to cool.

almond pastries with poached pears

35 g (1^1/4 oz) unsalted butter, chopped
40 g (1^1/2 oz) caster (superfine) sugar
55 g (^{1}/2 cup) ground almonds
3 egg yolks
^{1}/2 teaspoon natural vanilla extract
1 x 375 g (13 oz) packet puff pastry

to serve
poached pears (below)
vanilla ice cream

Preheat the oven to 220°C (425°F/Gas 7). Place the butter, sugar, almonds, 2 egg yolks and vanilla in a food processor and process until combined.

On a lightly floured surface, roll out the pastry until 3 mm (^{1}/4 inch) thick. Using a sharp knife, cut out two 25 x 10 cm (10 x 4 inch) rectangles. Lay one piece of pastry on a baking tray lined with baking paper. Prick the pastry base all over with a fork. Spoon over the almond mixture, leaving a 2 cm (^{3}/4 inch) border around the edges.

Place the second rectangle of pastry horizontally on a cutting board and, leaving a 2 cm (^{3}/4 inch) border, cut slashes 1 cm (^{1}/2 inch) apart.

Lightly beat the remaining egg yolk then brush the border of the first rectangle. Place the second pastry rectangle over the top and seal by lightly pressing the edges with your fingertips. Freeze for 15 minutes.

Brush the top of the pastry with the beaten egg yolk and place in the oven. Bake for 25 minutes, or until golden. Serve with poached pears and vanilla ice cream. Serves 6

poached pears

115 g (^{1}/2 cup) caster (superfine) sugar
2 pieces lemon zest

1 vanilla bean, split
6 small pears, peeled

Place the sugar, zest, vanilla bean and 750 ml (3 cups) water in a saucepan over a medium heat and stir until the sugar is dissolved. Bring to a simmer, add the pears, cover and cook for 10 minutes. Remove from the heat and stand, covered, for another 30 minutes. Remove the pears from the poaching liquid and serve.

I like to serve these puddings with crème fraîche. I find its gentle tang cuts the richness of the chocolate perfectly.

soft-centred chocolate puddings

200 g (7 oz) good-quality dark chocolate, chopped
100 g (3¹/2 oz) unsalted butter, chopped
3 eggs, lightly beaten
115 g (¹/2 cup) caster (superfine) sugar
2 tablespoons plain (all-purpose) flour

to serve
thick (double/heavy) cream or crème fraîche

Preheat the oven to 200°C (400°F/Gas 6). Place the chocolate and butter in a heatproof bowl over a saucepan of simmering water, making sure the bowl does not touch the water, and stir until just melted.

Place the eggs, sugar and flour in a bowl and mix until just combined. Gradually mix in the chocolate mixture. Pour the mixture into four 250 ml (1 cup) ovenproof ramekins and place on a baking tray. Bake until the edges are set, about 15 minutes. Serve with cream or crème fraîche. Serves 4

apple and almond puddings

150 g (5¹/2 oz) unsalted butter
150 g (5¹/2 oz) caster (superfine) sugar
3 Granny Smith apples, peeled, cored and sliced
1 teaspoon natural vanilla extract

batter

175 g (6 oz) unsalted butter, cubed
175 g (6 oz) caster (superfine) sugar
3 eggs
100 g (3¹/2 oz) almond meal
100 g (3¹/2 oz) plain (all-purpose) flour
2 teaspoons baking powder
1 teaspoon cinnamon

to serve

cream

Preheat the oven to 180°C (350°F/Gas 4). Place a saucepan over a medium to high heat and add the butter and sugar. Stir until the butter is melted and the sugar dissolved. Add the apple and vanilla and cook for 10 minutes, or until soft and caramelized.

To make the batter, cream the butter and sugar until pale and creamy. Add the eggs, one at a time, stirring until well combined. Fold in the almond meal, flour, baking powder and cinnamon and mix until combined.

Lightly grease and line six 250 ml (1 cup) ovenproof ramekins. Arrange the caramelized apples on the bottom. Divide the batter evenly between the ramekins and smooth over with the back of a spoon. Cook for about 25 minutes, or until lightly golden.

Run a knife around the edge of each ramekin then invert onto a serving dish. Serve with cream. Serves 6

This mousse is just as delicious with fresh passionfruit or crushed blackberries swirled in.

white chocolate mousse with raspberry ripple

250 g (9 oz) good-quality white chocolate, chopped
80 ml (1/3 cup) milk
1 teaspoon natural vanilla extract
3 eggs, separated
375 ml (1 1/2 cups) cream
250 g (1 punnet) raspberries

Place the white chocolate, milk and vanilla in a heatproof bowl over a saucepan of simmering water, making sure the bowl does not touch the water. Heat until the chocolate is just melted, stirring regularly. Allow to cool for 5 minutes. Add the egg yolks, beating well after each addition.

Whip the cream in a bowl until soft peaks form then fold through the chocolate mixture until just combined. Whisk the egg whites in a large, dry, clean stainless steel bowl until soft peaks form. Using a large metal spoon, fold through the chocolate mixture in two batches. Divide the mousse between six 250 ml (1 cup) serving dishes. Using a fork, crush the raspberries in a separate bowl then swirl over the top of the mousse. Cover and chill for 3 to 4 hours, or until set. Serves 6

bills library

One of my greatest pleasures is to be inspired by the cookbooks I read like novels. My consumption of cookbooks is second only to my consumption of food. I admire many great cookbook authors and these are a few of my favourites.

Amad, Abla, *The Lebanese Kitchen*, Viking, Melbourne, 2001

Alexander, Stephanie, *The Cook's Companion*, Viking, Melbourne, 1996

Beranbaum, Rose Levy, *The Pie And Pastry Bible*, Scribner, New York, 1998

Beranbaum, Rose Levy, *The Cake Bible*, William Morrow, New York, 1998

David, Elizabeth, *Elizabeth David Classics*, Grub Street, London, 1999

Dupleix, Jill, *New Food*, William Heinemann Australia, Melbourne, 1994

Dupleix, Jill, *Old Food*, Allen & Unwin, 1998

Hazan, Marcella, *The Classic Italian Cookbook*, Papermac, London, 1980

Hazan, Marcella, *The Essentials of Classic Italian Cooking*, Macmillan, London, 1992

Jamison, Cheryl Alters, and Jamison, Bill, *A Real American Breakfast*, William Morrow, New York, 2002

Perry, Neil, *Simply Asian*, Viking, Melbourne, 2000

Roden, Claudia, *The Food of Italy*, Vintage, London, 1999

Roden, Claudia, *Mediterranean Cookery*, BBC Books, London, 1987

Solomon, Charmaine, *Encyclopedia of Asian Food*, William Heinemann Australia, Melbourne, 1996

Time-Life Series, *The Good Cook Series*, Chief Consultant Richard Olney, Time-Life Books, Amsterdam, 1978–1982

Waters, Alice, *Chez Panisse Café Cookbook*, HarperCollins Publishers, New York, 1999

Waters, Alice, *Chez Panisse Desserts*, Random House, New York, 1985

Wells, Patricia, *At Home in Provence*, Kyle Cathie, London, 1998

Wells, Patricia, *Bistro*, Workman Publishing Company, New York, 1989

Wells, Patricia, *Trattoria*, Kyle Cathie, London, 1993

Wolfert, Paula, *The Cooking of the Eastern Mediterranean*, HarperCollins, New York, 1994

Wolfert, Paula, *Mediterranean Cooking*, HarperCollins, New York, 1994

Wolfert, Paula, *Mostly Mediterranean*, Penguin Books, New York, 1998

index